D1539289

"William Mills has given us a true story told truthfully, a story of a faith lost and found, a story of the church at its best and worst, a story of a priest who persisted in his vocation in spite of everything. Service to the Body of Christ, the church, is not for the faint of heart and yet, in the end, there are blessings."

—Will Willimon
United Methodist Bishop, retired, and Professor of the Practice of Christian Ministry, Duke Divinity School; author, *Who Lynched Willie Earle? Preaching to Confront Racism.*

"William Mills has gone honest and intimate with us in telling his story of the travail of ministry. His drama of mean-spirited *betrayal* in the congregation and the late unexpected *reassurance* of support replicates our best story of crucifixion and resurrection."

—Walter Brueggemann
Columbia Theological Seminary

"William Mills' memoir is a beautifully crafted, honest, wise, and insightful book. It stands in the very best tradition of spirituality—a writer and text that can speak to the real condition of the soul, and the day-to-day struggle that many have with belief. . . Honest and wise books on religious resilience are often hard to find. But this is one of those rare gems, and I commend it for anyone who knows how long our spiritual journey can be."

—Martyn Percy
Dean of Christ Church, Oxford

"The Church speaks a lot about truth but isn't so good at honesty. Here is a priest who has learned the cost of this and who, with courage and imagination, encourages us to join him and to say it as it is. We clergy often know the words of religion but miss the music. William Mills calls us back to the vocation of trying to tune our lives to the harmonies of the eternal but only by recognizing emotional and factual truth and in pursuit of justice. Enjoy it and feel yourself defrost."

—Mark Oakley
Dean, St. John's College, Cambridge

"*Losing My Religion* is the brave, tender, furious account of how William Mills is lifted, brought low, broken, healed, and made whole. As books about religious life go, it is among the wisest and most honest I've ever read. This book should keep company on your shelf with the better works of J.F. Powers, Larry Woiwode, and Thomas Merton."

—Kyle Minor
Author of *Praying Drunk: Stories*

"This book should be required reading for every seminarian of every confessional tradition, not as a warning, but as an invitation to assume with loving faithfulness the awesome task of ministry."

—John Breck
Retired Professor of New Testament and Ethics,
Saint Vladimir's Orthodox Theological Seminary

"Mills' honest journey from disorientation back to hope will inspire all who read this wonderfully rendered memoir."

—Scott Hoezee
Director, the Center for Excellence in Preaching, Calvin Theological Seminary

"For the clergy as well as the congregation, William Mills' memoir of parish ministry chronicles with refreshing honesty and insight the three-part journey from childhood to ordination to the perils of pastoral life."

—Robert Winstead
Assistant Professor of Pastoral Theology, Candler School of Theology

This is a work of substance and clarity. It is moving, poignant, funny, and inspiring. The memoir is entitled *Losing My Religion*, but it is a testament to all that can be gained by remaining true to one's moral compass, staying honest and authentic, seeking to learn lessons in each of life's challenges. In these pages, Mills inspires us to take what we are given and be transformed. This is a passionate, compelling book, full of meaning.

—Judy Goldman
Author, *Together: A Memoir of a Marriage and a Medical Mishap*

Losing My Religion

Losing My Religion

A Memoir of Faith and Finding

William C. Mills

RESOURCE *Publications* · Eugene, Oregon

LOSING MY RELIGION
A Memoir of Faith and Finding

Resource Publications
An Imprint of Wipf and Stock Publishers
199 W. 8th Ave., Suite 3
Eugene, OR 97401

www.wipfandstock.com

PAPERBACK ISBN: 978-1-5326-6373-4
HARDCOVER ISBN: 978-1-5326-6374-1
EBOOK ISBN: 978-1-5326-6375-8

Cataloguing-in-Publication data:

Names: Mills, William, C.

Title: Book losing my religion : a memoir of faith and finding / William C. Mills.

Description: Eugene, OR: Resource Publications, 2019 | Includes bibliographical references.

Identifiers: ISBN 978-1-5326-6373-4 (paperback) | ISBN 978-1-5326-6374-1 (hardcover) | ISBN 978-1-5326-6375-8 (ebook)

Subjects: LCSH: Pastoral Ministry | Spiritual Memoir | Clergy Memoir | Eastern Orthodox Church — Clergy

Manufactured in the U.S.A.   01/11/19

With Gratitude

George and Gordon Jacobs

Tom O' Neal

and

The Davidson Clergy Center Staff

"Write in a book what you see and send it to the seven churches."

—Revelation 1:10

"Behold, I send you out as sheep in the midst of wolves; so be wise as serpents and innocent as doves."

—Matthew 10:16

"The Church is a whore, but she's also your mother."

—Attributed to Saint Augustine, 4th Century

Contents

Author Statement

M any events in this book took place more than twelve years ago and were condensed for the sake of retelling the narrative. Certain names have been changed to protect identities. The dialogue reflects the sentiment of what transpired and is not exact. A memoir is a collection of memories filtered through time and experience and is not a work of history.

Preface

I'm a priest. Not just any priest, but an Eastern Orthodox priest. I'm in charge of a congregation, which is also called a parish. People in the parish are called parishioners, and they call me Father. No, I'm not their *biological* Father, I'm their *spiritual* Father, but I don't feel very spiritual, at least most of the time. I have plenty of doubts about ministry, about God, and about the Church. To make life simple, I usually introduce myself as a pastor rather than a priest, since priest sounds Catholic and a lot of people don't like Catholics, at least not here in the South. If I say *priest* they immediately follow up with, "Then why do you wear a ring?" I tell them I wear a ring because I'm married and have two kids. That confuses them even more. This is annoying because then I need to explain that even though both Catholics and Orthodox use the term *priest,* Orthodox priests are permitted to get married and have children, but Catholic priests cannot. Well, at least in theory. I don't have, the energy or the interest to go through this rigmarole every time, so I usually say I'm a pastor and leave it at that.

Throughout my working life I have been called a lot of things: parson, pastor, preacher, minister, vicar, chaplain, reverend, cleric, man of the cloth, and just plain "Bill" by an evangelical conservative Christian who didn't like titles. When I put out my hand he barely wanted to shake it. Why can he call his Churchy friends brother and sister but he can't call me *Father*? What's up with that?

My other title is rector. A rector is a fancy name for a priest who is in charge of a parish. So theoretically I'm a priest who is also a father and a rector. Now to make matters even more complicated I also have a doctorate in theology, and sometimes I use the title Doctor before my name. So some people call me Reverend Doctor Father or Reverend Father Doctor, and some just don't know what to call me. Clergy have way too many fancy titles, if you ask me. So maybe the hardcore evangelical conservative Christian guy was right just calling me "Bill." That's fine by me.

My friends ask me what I do all day and I tell them that I wear a lot of black and drink lots of coffee. They don't believe me but it's true. I spend more time in Starbucks than the store manager. Most of the time I meet parishioners and we talk. Actually they talk and I listen. So I sit and listen to pains and problems, trials and tribulations; and sometimes stories so horrific that I want to go home and throw up. I don't feel like I'm doing much, but they tell me they feel better after talking with me. I hear more confessions over coffee than I do in church. Over the years I've learned that people don't like meeting in church. It reminds them too much of God. People open up when they don't have all that religion shoved in their face. Anyway, the chairs in church are hard and the coffee isn't great. Maybe we should buy comfy chairs and brew better coffee?

But, honestly, I do more than just drink coffee. I officiate at the Sunday Eucharist, preach sermons, baptize naked infants, perform marriages (not naked), bury the dead, visit the sick and suffering, encourage the faint-hearted, and reprove the wayward. In addition to all of that I also teach adult class, hear confessions (slightly boring), write the weekly bulletin (very boring), attend meetings (extremely boring). Visiting the sick and the dying ranks pretty high up on my list and I'd much rather visit the sick and dying than perform weddings. At weddings no one cares what I'm doing, their eyes are fixed on the bride and her dress. At funerals everyone's worried about *their* future so they make sure to listen. In my book: funerals good, weddings bad.

According to our model pastor, Saint Paul, I'm supposed to be all things to all people, and often I don't know whether I'm coming or going. Actually I feel like I'm failing most of the time. For some reason I don't think Saint Paul had to write weekly bulletins and attend meetings. He was lucky. But he did spend a lot of time writing letters. Speaking of letters, I forgot to mention that I also get the mail, order candles, and purchase wine. You should see the cashier lady when I buy ten bottles of Taylor Port. She probably thinks I'm saucing it up on Saturday nights.

In the past I have been known to take out the garbage, arrange flowers, unclog a toilet or two, and shovel snow. I've also washed windows, trimmed trees, and cleaned up condoms from the parking lot. I don't want parishioners seeing *those* on Sunday morning. Now that we hired a cleaning service, most of my janitorial work is done. I still unclog a toilet or two and thanks to our new parking lot gate I'm no longer on condom patrol, at least for now.

For eighteen years I have served as the rector of The Nativity of the Holy Virgin Orthodox Church, in Charlotte, North Carolina. The official name is the *Nativity of the Holy Theotokos Orthodox Church*. It barely fits on my business card. The congregation is located on a busy road and my hunch is that people driving by have no idea what "Nativity" or "Theotokos" means. When was the last time you heard the word Theotokos? Never, right? Nativity is an old word for "birth" and Theotokos is an ancient Greek word that means "God-bearer." We believe that Mary gave birth to Jesus, who is the Son of God. Orthodox are known to like old and traditional things, so we kept the name Theotokos rather than Virgin Mary. I wish we could change the name to Saint Mary's but the bishop won't like that. I bet you more people would recognize Saint Mary's than Theotokos.

Eighteen years is somewhat of a record. According to national studies the average tenure of a parish minister is just around five years. Why you may ask? Well, would you want to work crazy hours, have little free time with your family, hear about people's pains and problems, attend meetings, and talk about God all the time? Probably not. According to statistics by now I should be a hospital chaplain, postal worker, teacher, librarian, garbage collector, landscaper, truck driver, or a pastoral counselor, but not a pastor. I almost didn't make it.

Twelve years ago my parish imploded, or exploded, however you want to think of it, when a third of the congregation left in a public power play. That happens a lot in parishes, big fish in small ponds don't do well. We had a few too many big fish. I was devastated. I never imagined that this would happen. No one does. After four years of college and six years of seminary, I was ready to lead a parish. Or so I thought. Marva Dawn, a noted writer of spirituality and ministry, said that being a pastor is like being peppered with popcorn, after a while you just get tired, pack your bags, and move on. Most smart ones do. I'm either too stubborn or too stupid, so I stayed. This is my story.

Acknowledgements

This book would not have been possible without the incredible Davidson Clergy Center staff, especially George Jacobs and Tom O' Neal who showed me the light and led me towards healing and wholeness.

I'm indebted to my writing teachers, especially Kyle Minor who started me on this journey and gave me the inspiration to finish it and to the ever gracious Judy Goldman who provided suggestions that made this book a much better project. To Michael Breck, whose keen editorial eyes made me a much better writer than I am. Everyone needs a good editor in their corner.

I also must thank the Collegeville Ecumenical and Cultural Research Institute, The Gotham Writing Workshop, The Great Smokey Mountains Writing Program, Table Rock Writers Workshop, and the North Carolina Writers Network, where I had the chance to workshop some of the chapters in this book.

To my dear friends and readers, Adam DeVille, Nicholas Denysenko, Michael Kallas, Paul Kritzer, and Michael Plekon who were there every step of the way, provided feedback and encouragement.

To my Nativity family, both living and departed, who continue to support me and thankfully overlook my numerous shortcomings. I'm honored to serve this special community of faith.

To the Wipf and Stock team who took on this project.

To my spiritual parents, Father Paul and Barbara Kucynda and Father John and Barbara Ealy, words cannot express my sincere gratitude.

For Mom and Dad, thanks for everything. What more can I say?

Finally to my family, Taisia, Hannah, and Emma for their care and compassion, love and much laughter. You are my rock and my foundation. I couldn't have written this book without you.

Pentecost 2018

PART ONE

CHAPTER I

Serve the Lord With Gladness

Most of my friends attended Church once a month. We went twice a week, five times during Lent. Every Saturday afternoon around four o'clock Mom stood on our front porch in Maplewood, New Jersey, dressed in her baby blue satin muumuu sans bra and girdle yelling,

"Billy, Billy," the sound of her bellowing voice echoing down the street.

Nothing worse than your mom calling while you're playing with friends.

I'd yell back, "What Ma?"

"Come home, we gotta go to Church," she'd yell back.

I couldn't hear, so she'd yell again, "Come home, we gotta go to Church."

By that time everyone on the block heard her. When she finished she would wave her arms back and forth over her head as if she was sending an SOS signal. Then she'd turn around and walk back inside.

And with that I'd drop the pick-up soccer game and high-tail it up the block. Mom never called twice. When she said jump, I asked how high. When she said, "let's go," she meant *now*, not in five minutes. Her friends called her Sonia Begonia, I called her Leo the Lion.

Arriving home I would take a quick shower, brush my teeth, squirt a few spritzes of Drakkar Noir on my neck, comb my hair, and put on my Church clothes: khaki pants, a polo shirt, dress socks, and dark brown Sperry Topsiders. No jeans and certainly no sneakers. "Billy, we're going to

God's House, not the Pancake House," she'd say if she caught me wearing my white Converse high tops.

As soon as she backed out of the driveway she'd turn the radio dial to 1500AM, the Jimmy Sturr Polka Hour. For the next thirty minutes we listened to polkas from around the world, from the *Beer Barrel Polka* to the *Pennsylvania Polka, Too Fat For Me Polka,* and the *Licorice Stick Polka.* If Mom was in a good mood she'd start tapping her hand on the steering wheel in time with the three-step beat. If Purgatory existed, this was it: a fourteen-year-old sitting in a locked car listening to Frank Yankovic and Lazlo Popovich's latest top ten polka hits. I often prayed that the radio would break, but God never answered that one.

I couldn't complain too much because she always gave me a choice, either Jimmy Sturr or Church music. She kept not just *one* but *two* small cases worth of liturgical music in the back seat. She had it all, the Divine Liturgy in English and Slavonic (an ancient form of Russian), Matins, Vespers, the Funeral Service, the Wedding service, Christmas, Easter, and Holy Week. I had the entire liturgical year at my fingertips. Once in a while I'd ask her to put in the Slavonic Divine Liturgy just so I didn't have to listen to one more version of the *Beer Barrel Polka.* If she put in the funeral service she'd start singing along and about halfway through she'd start tearing up. I didn't like seeing Mom cry like that. No one wants to see their mom cry. She enjoyed her music, and me, well, my mind was somewhere else, usually on girls that I wanted to date or on the growing pile of homework still sitting on my desk. I hated the fact that we were always the first to arrive,

"There's no one else here, just us," I'd say.

"I know, I know, I wanted to make sure we weren't late," she'd say while parking the car.

"Late? Vespers begins at six." Looking down at my watch I could see that it was only five thirty.

She'd turn to me, "Billy, you never know about traffic. Now stop. We can sit here quietly until Father Paul opens up."

So there we'd sit, just the two of us, staring at the grass and the oak trees across the lawn. Sometimes she'd keep the radio on listening to her polkas.

Then on my side of the car I'd turn and see Father Paul Kucynda walk out of the rectory, across the parking lot, and then up the Church steps. He'd be dressed in his usual ankle-length black cassock, wearing a gold cross around his neck, the cross swinging back and forth as he climbed the steps. He'd turn his head slightly over in our direction and wave. When he walked he'd pick up the front part of his cassock like a lady would pick up part of her evening dress so as not to trip over it.

"Come on Billy," Mom would say, "Church's open, lets go."

Before exiting the car she'd reach into her pocket book and take out a thin tube of red lipstick and look over at me and smile, "Gotta look alive." She'd maneuver the container around her lips making sure not to get any on her cheeks and then lightly dab them with a tissue. She'd glance in the mirror making sure there were no smudges, fix her hair, and then drop the container in her pocketbook. Mom wasn't much for makeup but she did put some on for work and for Church. She'd take out a small white can of Binaca breath spray, spray two spritzes in her mouth and offer me some. I'd spray twice and give it back, feeling a stinging sensation on the tip of my tongue.

We attended Holy Resurrection Orthodox Church, in Wayne, a leafy-tree-lined suburb in northeastern New Jersey. The congregation was established in the mid-60's during a time of booming missions and parishes in this part of New Jersey. When you drove into the parking lot you got a sense of presence and permanence, with a beautiful carved sign and brick building greeting you. I had two homes, my home in Maplewood and my spiritual home at Holy Resurrection.

We'd slowly walk along the sidewalk and up the stairs into the narthex, which is the entry area. A large floor-to-ceiling painted mural of Jesus' baptism in the Jordan River greeted us in the vestibule. Holy Resurrection was modest compared with older Orthodox Churches that had bell towers, parish halls, and were decorated with hand-painted icons from floor to ceiling. Holy Resurrection had white painted walls with small wooden icons and the ceiling was comprised of exposed wooden beams which gave the interior a rustic look. Our parish had a simple elegance to it, decorated but not gaudy, modern yet traditional.

The Church is dark. The lights on the wrought iron chandeliers are on low and the mood is subdued as we wait for the service to begin. Mom takes out several one-dollar bills and puts them in the wicker basket on the candle desk. Michael and his dad stand behind the desk welcoming people as they come in. Michael has Down's Syndrome and rocks back and forth, occasionally grunting. Mom stops and says hello to Michael and hugs him. I quickly walk past, avoiding eye contact, and never shake his hand, thinking that Down's Syndrome is contagious.

Mom takes the candles from Michael gives me two and we walk up the center aisle and make the Orthodox sign of the cross over our chests: forehead, middle of chest, right shoulder, left shoulder, and kiss the main icon in the center of the Church. We walk a few feet ahead to our right and kiss the icon of Jesus, light a candle and then walk directly to our left and kiss the icon of the Virgin Mary and light a candle. We then walk back to our family pew, the third one from the back. The wood pews are cold and hard. We both kneel and silently recite our prayers together, ending with the *Lord's Prayer*. We again cross ourselves three times, and then sit down.

I liked sitting in the quiet Church. At home there was constant noise; the sound of cars passing by our busy street, the clanking of our forced steam heater in the winter, and the low hum of the air conditioner in the summer. Here, it's completely quiet except for the back door opening and closing. I'd sit there and watch the older ladies walk in and venerate the icons, very few men attended. Some looked like they had a hard life. Makeup hides a lot, but not everything. These women suffered; wars, domestic disputes, resentments, ungrateful children, and lost dreams; some had buried their husbands, others had buried their children. They were strong, survivors all of them.

I watch Father Paul walk behind the Altar. Orthodox Churches have an icon screen which is called an iconostasis that is usually made from wood and separates the Altar area from the rest of the Church. The iconostasis in our parish is wrought iron so you can see through it to the Altar area. Father Paul looks important as he lights the seven red votive candles on the Altar table. Father Paul is tall, black hair and slightly balding, and wears gold-rimmed classes. By now he's been in ministry for more than a decade; the same services, the same routine, week after week, year after year. While classmates, neighbors, and teachers have come and gone, Father Paul is the one constant person in my life.

He exits the Altar, walks out in front of the icon screen and lights all the candles there: the one in front of the large icon of Jesus, the one in front of the Virgin Mary. While I'm watching him, Mom sorts through her pocketbook and takes out her slender *Reader's Digest* calendar looking at future appointments or making a grocery list. After he's done lighting candles, he walks down the far aisle near our pew and stops.

"Hi, Sonia," Father Paul greets Mom.

"Hello, Father Paul." She nudges me. "Hello," I say reluctantly. I'd rather just sit there quietly. Talking is an effort.

Father Paul looks over in my direction and offers his hand. I shake it. "How's school going?"

"Fine." I say looking down at my hands. I don't know what else to say.

Mom interjects, "Billy's got all Bs this term and a few As. Isn't that right Billy?" She nudges me again with her elbow. Now I'm embarrassed. She was always telling people about how well I was doing in school. I realize that she's proud of me but at the same time I'd rather not have the whole world know about my private life.

"That's great. You gotta keep it up, especially if you want to go to college," he says.

"Yeah, that's what Mom says."

I look at her for affirmation. She nods. Mom attended two years of nursing school and dad barely graduated from high school. Her life was limited, coming to age at the early stages of the women's movement she missed out on the bra burning, protests, and sit-ins. She basically had three choices: secretary, teacher, or nurse. She had high hopes for her son's life, that it would be better than hers.

"Well, I need an Altar server tonight, you wanna serve?"

"Sure," I say.

I look over at Mom for permission and she nods telling me that it's okay.

Father Paul gets up and walks away towards the Altar and I follow, making the usual full prostration on the floor when entering. I bow reverently, cross myself and walk over to the sacristy room, where the liturgical robes, candles, incense, charcoal, prayer books, pamphlets, and wine are kept. Twice a week for eight years I would walk into that same room with its natural smells of beeswax mixed with hints of rose, lilac, and jasmine. It feels comfortable here. It suits my personality. While everyone else sits on the other side of the iconostasis, I'm here, sitting in the inner sanctum, the holy of holies, taking care of God's house. I feel at home.

The Altar server robes hang in the closet and are color-coordinated with Father Paul's vestments: gold for the part of the year we call "ordinary time," maroon for Advent, purple for Lent, white for Eastertide, green for Pentecost, and blue for the feasts of the Virgin Mary. I like the change of colors, it reminds me of the four seasons: winter, spring, summer, fall; a rhythm, change of weather, change of life. The Church year has a cycle too, every season a new theme, a new beginning. My favorite robes are white. They look clean and fresh, shining with their silver trim. Even today I like to wear white at the Easter night vigil, they look beautiful under the bright lights.

After neatly folding my robe into a square, I present it to Father Paul for a blessing. He makes a large sign of the cross over the gold-embossed cross and I kiss his hand, which smells of Dove soap. If there is time before the service, Father Paul sits next to me in the sacristy asking me about my parents, about school, about my favorite subjects. He shows interest in my life. I notice that his breath smells clean and fresh. Sometimes we just sit there on the folding chairs looking out the window in silence. Sometimes we talk about upcoming Church holidays or special youth group projects.

Father Paul never pushed me to peruse seminary studies or enter the ministry. He was a quiet stable presence in my life, always there when I needed to talk. He was the father that I never had, the father that I always wanted. His glasses, watch, vestments, and book-lined office were impressive to a young boy. His college and seminary diplomas hung in fancy frames in his home office. Father Paul had a real job, an important job. He worked for God. Every week he led us in prayer. I watched him as he baptized babies and buried the dead. People came to him for confession and advice. He was the local God expert. I wanted to be like Father Paul. I wanted to be important.

My father was a transporter at Saint Barnabas Hospital in nearby Livingston and in the hospital hierarchy he was one level above janitor. His job was simple: he took patients from one part of the hospital to another; from admitting to their room, from their room to surgery, from surgery to ICU, and sometimes from ICU to the morgue. He took medication from the pharmacy to the floor unit clerk, and x-rays from radiology to pathology. My dad didn't have floor-to-ceiling bookshelves or a computer. He didn't wear fancy clothes or a gold cross. He certainly didn't have college diplomas hanging in the house. He wore a white uniform and his office was the break room where he enjoyed his Camels and strong black coffee. He was Dad to me and Donnie to his friends. He was a lot of things, but he was nothing like Father Paul.

At six o'clock the bells ring and Vespers begins. I take my place a few feet from the Altar table. My job is to watch Father Paul and see if he needs anything. I'm like a waiter at an expensive restaurant making sure the patrons have all that they need. When I give him the censer he makes the sign of the cross with it in front of the Altar and then walks counterclockwise around, censing each side of the table three times, bowing his head each time. Gentle puffs of lilac-scented smoke rise in the air. When he's finished censing he chants in a loud voice, "Blessed is our God always now and forever and unto ages of ages," which echoes throughout the congregation, and the choir responds with a loud, "Amen." The choir starts singing Psalm 104, the psalm of creation.

Some people ask me when I wanted to become a priest. I really don't know. There was never one of those thunderbolt or Hollywood moments that you see in movies. The sky didn't open, nor did I hear voices. There was never a time when I found Jesus or that I felt a special pull to ministry. Looking back I can say that I always had a sense of calling and service. A lot of it had to do with those quiet times sitting with Father Paul in the Altar. Probably a lot has to do with my parents. They both worked in the hospital and devoted themselves to serving others. They instilled in me hard work and excellence in all that I do. On Christmas Day 1981, my first day serving in the Altar, Father Paul gave me a small black Divine Liturgy book. He inscribed it with the following words:

> *Dear Bill:*
>
> *Today is the beginning of your service in the Lord's Altar. May you serve the Lord with joy and gladness all the days of your life.*
>
> *With love in Christ,*
>
> *Father Paul*

The pages are now onion-skin thin and yellowing. I have used this prayer book every Sunday for the past thirty-two years. Back then I never thought I'd be standing in front of an Altar table just like the one at Holy Resurrection. It's funny how life turns out: seeds planted over thirty years ago are planted again in the next generation in hope, that they will bear fruit. I think of all of the other Altar servers that served with me who eventually became lawyers, doctors, scientists, teachers, mechanics, bankers, but not pastors. We attended the same Church school classes, and went on the same Altar boy retreats, yet I became a pastor and they didn't. But it was there, in that sacristy room, over those small quiet conversations that I was inspired to enter into priestly ministry.

CHAPTER 2

I Can't Get Away from Jesus

There was never a time when Jesus wasn't around. I mean *never*. He was everywhere: at Church, in our living room, in the kitchen, in my bedroom, and even in our car. He was everywhere but the bathroom, and I often wondered if he'd appear there too. I couldn't get away from him. Like the prophet Jonah I tried running away but he followed me wherever I went.

We lived in a 1920s two-bedroom house with a detached wood garage and postage-stamp front yard. The front door opened into the living room. Some called it cute, I called it crowded. It was two stories plus a basement and two-tone green siding. The bottom part was dark green and the top part was lighter green, and according to Mom it was *vomit green*. On the inside front wall, behind Dad's brown Barcalounger chair, hung a gilded Byzantine-style icon of Jesus with flowing brown hair. Dad's chair faced our television set and I always thought Jesus was watching TV too. In our kitchen, above our back door, hung a circular wooden icon of the Last Supper. Thankfully it wasn't one of those velvet Michelangelo look-alike paint by numbers that you see at garage sales.

To the left of the kitchen was our dining room and on the wall above the light switch, hung a license-plate-sized baby-blue glass picture of praying hands engraved with the words, "*Slava Isusu Christu*," which is a Slavonic phrase: "Glory to Jesus Christ."

One of the most intimate memories I have is kneeling at the length of the bed, decked out in my favorite Star Wars bedspread. I knelt there night after night in my red flannel pajamas and prayed to God, holding my hands tightly together while looking upon the white plastic cross that hung above my pillow. Across from my bed, on the shelf above my heater were several icons of the Virgin Mary and various saints. Many traditional icons have piercing eyes and I remember thinking that my icons were watching me. One of the special icons that we had in our house was my grandfather's icon of Jesus that was encased in gold. Decades later when I was a young pastor I overheard an angry mom threaten her unruly son, "You know Johnny, Jesus is watching you so you better be good." Unfortunately over the years I'd hear other mom's threaten their children in the same way. No wonder some people have a messed up image of God.

Although we had a lot of icons we didn't have books. Mom would walk with me the three blocks to the Maplewood Public Library where she'd take me to story time. I became a voracious reader and often read by flashlight under the covers. Being an only child I was drawn to reading. Books became my friends and my guides in life, and kept me busy especially when my friends were away on vacation. I especially enjoyed the *Hardy Boys Series*. Dad read the *Farmers Almanac* and *Reader's Digest*. Mom read the *Ladies Home Journal, Good Housekeeping,* and the annual Sears catalog which was the size of a telephone book. I eagerly awaited its arrival because I would dog-ear the pages with all the toys and clothes I wanted for my birthday and Christmas. There was also a black leather King James Bible on our coffee table. I don't recall either Mom or Dad reading it, I never did. It just sat there on the table until I had to move it when I helped Mom clean the house. Today when visiting families I often see a Bible on the coffee table and wonder whether or not they read it. My hunch is that they don't. I can tell too, the pages are crisp and clean and the spine doesn't look worn.

It's customary in the Orthodox Church to have your home blessed during the feast of Epiphany, which is the commemoration of Jesus' baptism in the Jordan River. The priest blesses water at Church, and then takes the holy water to each of the families in the congregation and blesses their house with it. Home blessings are a way to rededicate one's life to God and to be reminded that all creation is sacred and holy.

Every January Father Paul would bless our house. Mom looked forward to his visit, but I didn't. Maplewood was a small bedroom community and Springfield Avenue divided the town in half. On our side of Springfield Avenue the homes were small and modest, with single car garages and small yards. The other side of Springfield Avenue the homes were larger and more stately; wrap-around porches and large front yards with concrete walkways. While walking to school I imagined that I lived in one of those homes rather than mine. They had three or four bedrooms, ours only had two. Father Paul lived in a parish-owned rectory with an office, formal living room, TV room, and furnished basement and I didn't want him seeing our small house, which was on the other side of the tracks.

Mom would make me help her clean, I should say, *scour* the house from top to bottom: "Now Billy, don't forget to move the furniture when you vacuum upstairs." I nodded to please her but never moved the furniture. What she didn't know wouldn't hurt her. Since we had a small house it didn't take long, but she wanted it spotless, "I don't want my priest thinking we live in a dump," she'd say, or, "We don't live in a pig sty." I can still picture her saying that with her newly wet hair up in curlers, rushing from room to room. When Mom cleaned, she was like a hurricane dusting, wiping, and shining everything in sight.

Then she would start cooking. She would make enough food for a family of ten: scrambled eggs and toast, bacon and sausage, and fresh fruit salad and coffee. She might have some donuts too, or a coffee cake or Danish that she'd pick up at the local Entenmann's warehouse. Dad would run over to Tabatchnik's Deli and get a dozen bagels and some smoked salmon.

She'd make me help her set the table. I'd start putting out the dishes. "No, not those. Use the *good china*, not that everyday ware." She spoke like she was the lady of the house preparing dinner for the Queen of England. For a family that didn't entertain she had three sets of china: her everyday ware, of which she had two kinds, and then her *special* china, which she used only on Christmas, Thanksgiving, and Easter, and kept in a special sideboard in the dining room. She made a big fuss about setting the table: "Now Billy, forks on the left and knives and spoons on the right, hear me?" She yelled from the kitchen. I yelled back, "Yeah, Ma, sure." I didn't care. I was jealous that dad wasn't helping. He always said the deli was busy but I bet he took his sweet time on purpose. I would have liked to escape from under Mom's radar too for a while.

When the doorbell rang, she quickly surveyed the table, every square inch was filled with either dinnerware or food. When she was satisfied, she looked around and gave a small nod that everything was okay. She then went into the kitchen to get some matches and light the center candle. She was finished.

Looking back I didn't realize why Mom went through all this trouble for Father Paul's visit. For Mom, Father Paul was one level below God. After all, week after week, year after year, she saw him up at the Altar in his priestly vestments leading us in prayer. She heard him speak about God. He was the one who heard our confessions and gave us communion. Father Paul wasn't just another person in our life, he was the God-man and for the God-man to come over for brunch, well, that was a big deal. Today I realize many people see me in this way and they too, like Mom, go to great lengths preparing for my visit. It's one thing to see clergy Sunday morning, but quite another to have us up close and personal in their dining room.

We never talked about God, the Church, or spirituality. I never saw either of my parents pray, but from our conversations and their actions, I knew deep down that they were devoted to helping those in need. Mom would call a sick parishioner or send a sympathy card to someone who lost a loved one. On more than one occasion she stopped to visit a friend in the hospital. No matter how tired she was she always took time to visit. She might have a quick bite of dinner and then make a few phone calls to those who were sick. She would go out and buy a small bouquet of flowers and a box of chocolates and bring them to a friend who was homebound. Mom and Dad didn't talk about their faith, they lived it.

Our life revolved around the rituals and routines of the Church year. On the Feast of the Transfiguration Mom brought a bowl of fresh fruit to Church to be blessed. At the Feast of the Dormition of the Virgin Mary she brought a vase of flowers to be blessed. We even attended Church on vacation. A few times I attempted to feign sickness, usually a headache or a stomachache in order to get out of going to services, but her usual response was, "You're fine. If I don't see either blood or bone you're okay." I never questioned why we went to so many services, it was just a part of our life.

Along with Church school I sang in the choir, served as a lector, and later participated in the parish youth group. My entire social life revolved around the Church. Every December the youth group spent the better part of Saturday in the Church basement making Christmas wreaths that we would sell as a fundraiser. At the end of the wreath-making session we had pizza and Father Paul would hear our confessions. On Holy Friday evening the youth group conducted a "lock in" where we all brought our sleeping bags and took turns reading from the Psalms over the tomb of Christ. We slept in the Church basement and then attended the Divine Liturgy the next morning. If given the choice I would have said no. Well, actually I did say no a few times, but Mom never took no for an answer. It was like that a lot. All I wanted was some freedom, to make some choices for myself. I learned early on not to speak up. I survived by avoiding conflict. Avoiding conflict isn't healthy. Life includes conflict, something that I learned the hard way.

I liked to be alone. I would get on my black and red Huffy bike and take long rides through town, peddling all the way to Maplecrest Park and back. I would be gone for a few hours, each time going a little further than before. Part of me wanted to keep going and not come back. I felt free. Free from my house and free from Mom. Maybe that's why Dad spent so much time in the garden, he was avoiding my mother.

In Middle School I made the local town soccer team. I enjoyed playing soccer and would play with my friends. We'd play after school well into the early evening. Since I was the tallest boy on the team I played goalkeeper, "Aye, Billy, you're a tall boy now, not like those wee ones over there," Mr. MacFarland, our soccer coach, told me in his thick Scottish brogue. When he changed practices from weeknights to Saturday afternoons, I'd knew I'd have problems on the home front.

One day Mom and I were driving home from practice and she said, "You have to tell Mr. MacFarland that you can't play anymore." She looked straight ahead while driving, "We have Vespers." "But Mom. . ." She interrupted, "No buts. Tell him next practice." Case closed. That's how most of our conversations went.

I was jealous of Mark and Roy whose parents let them go away for weekend Scouting trips and I couldn't play soccer because of a few Saturday practices? I wanted Dad to intervene, but I never asked him. It was useless. When Mom said no, she was unmovable. He was passive and when he did speak up a fight ensued.

One night, in a fit of anger, I started packing a large duffel bag with clothes, shoes, and a few books. I sat on my bed thinking of an escape plan. I couldn't drive so that was out of the question. I could walk to the train station, hop on a train to Manhattan. Then what? Where would I go? I was too young to get a hotel room. There was no way I was going to sleep in Central Park. I could walk down to Jerry's house, but that was a few blocks away, not far enough. Other kids ran away, but I was too chicken. I unpacked my bags and stayed. The feeling never left.

Yet somehow this Church thing had a hold of me. When I was very young I played priest. I put on my maroon terry cloth bathrobe and took a golden tassel from our living room draperies and used that as a belt. I set up a play altar at the coffee table with a plate and a cup and chanted some mumbo-jumbo pretending that I was Father Paul. Neither Mom nor Dad encouraged me. It happened naturally. I eventually learned that this behavior is not uncommon with children, they mimic what they see. On Sunday morning children might pick their nose or look out the window or play on the carpet, but somehow the symbolic world of liturgy; the hymns, prayers, and liturgical actions are communicated to our little ones.

I never distinguished the secular from the sacred, it was all one seamless whole. I attended school Monday through Friday and then we would go to Church every Saturday and Sunday. We did this all year long, including summers. During the six weeks of Lent we had to go to Church on Wednesday and Friday nights. On Wednesday night we attended an evening communion service called the Presanctified Liturgy. The Church was dark and lit with candles. We sang psalms and hymns. At the end we had communion. After the service we went to a local Greek diner for supper. On Fridays we attended a memorial service for the dead. Families gave names of their deceased relatives and Father Paul prayed for them. Mom always cried during this service especially at the singing of the solemn hymn, "Memory Eternal." Both of her parents died when she was in her early thirties. She was an only child and was responsible for their end-of-life care in addition to working a full time job as well as being a Mom.

Every Sunday during Lent we had Mission Vespers. Local parishes took turns hosting this evening service. Because the service was at four o'clock there wasn't enough time to go home which meant that we would drive to either the local mall or go grocery shopping. After the hour-long service the host priest delivered a sermon and then we all went downstairs to the basement and had refreshments: coffee, tea, cookies, and small cakes. There's nothing worse for a ten-year-old than to spend all day at Church, standing around, listening to Mom with her lady friends prattle about work, domestic life, or in the case of the older ladies, their health problems or deceased husbands. Over time resentment and anger built up. A little Church was fine, but too much Church, well, too much is sometimes too much.

Life came to a halt during Holy Week. Holy Week is a special time in the Church year, we follow Jesus during his last days: his entrance into Jerusalem, the Last Supper, his betrayal, trial, crucifixion, and finally on Easter Sunday his resurrection from the dead. During Holy Week our family attended twelve Church services, which translated into driving two hundred and sixty miles, thirty-six dollars in tolls, and thirteen hours in the car. Now that's a lot of services.

Our Holy Week marathon began on Lazarus Saturday morning, the day we commemorate Jesus raising Lazarus from the dead. It's customary for children to go to confession before the Lazarus Saturday Divine Liturgy, and afterwards everyone went downstairs to have a special pancake breakfast. The smell of the yeasty pancakes being cooked during the service was tempting. We couldn't wait to run downstairs knowing that there'd be stacks upon stacks of freshly made pancakes, gallons of orange juice, and carafes of syrup. After the breakfast we drove home and rested up until we had to return a few hours later for the Vespers of Palm Sunday, when Father Paul would bless palms and pussy willows.

On Holy Thursday, before the evening service, Dad mixed up a batch of my grandma's special egg bread, similar to challah or babka. I loved the sweet smell of the flour, warm milk, yeast, and sugar. Later that evening Dad punched down the dough, put it into three medium-sized round bread pans, and baked it in the oven. During the last five minutes of baking he'd brush the tops with an egg, milk, and sugar mixture. I still remember the dark shiny tops of bread when it came out of the oven. After the Holy Saturday Divine Liturgy we came home and Mom would make her famous potato salad and Dad would run down to Saint John the Baptist Ukrainian Catholic Church in Newark and pick up a few pounds of smoked kielbasa and cold pork roast. When Dad was out, I helped Mom dye one or two-dozen red eggs. The hardboiled egg is an ancient symbol of Jesus' tomb, the shell representing the tomb or grave and the egg itself representing new life. These eggs were later given out to the congregation by Father Paul after the Easter service.

Mom always said that the Easter vigil was the Orthodox version of the Super Bowl, it was the biggest day of our year. After all, how can you top Jesus being raised from the dead? The service began in a dark Church illuminated by a few candles. After the choir sang several hymns, Father Paul would come out of the Altar wearing his white vestments and holding the three-branched golden Easter candle signaling that the procession around the Church would start. We would walk around the Church and then stop at the front doors when Father Paul would read a Resurrection gospel and then greet us with the traditional Easter greeting: "Christ is Risen!" Everyone responded, "Indeed He is Risen!" He did this in English, Romanian,

Slavonic, and in Greek. After the third time he would knock on the front doors, two ushers would open them and we'd enter the Church, which was decorated with white Easter lilies and small pink and purple azalea bushes. I loved the fresh spring smell of the flowers and shrubs. At various times in the service Father Paul would walk down the center aisle between the pews swinging the silver censer with bells jingling and little wafts of sweet-smelling incense rising, all the time shouting, "Christ is Risen! "And the people responding, "Indeed He is Risen!" The night seemed like it lasted forever.

The service ended around one o'clock in the morning and we'd all go downstairs and Father Paul would walk around the hall blessing Easter baskets. After he was done we would sit down together and share our food. The smell was overpowering—table after table of baskets filled with smoked sausage, ham, pork roasts, homemade farmers cheese, hard boiled eggs, freshly baked breads, and sweet desserts. People brought along wine, beer, and vodka to share too. Some of the older women made *pysanky*, the Ukrainian-style decorated eggs and would give one to Father Paul. When I was older I wondered what a stranger would think of all of us crazy Christians eating kielbasa and roast pork sandwiches while swigging Stoli and Miller Lite at two o'clock in the morning.

Even though Jesus invaded my life, Mom gave me a great gift and exposed me to other faith traditions, especially Judaism. She worked for a Jewish boss and several of our family friends were Jewish. Maplewood had two synagogues and many of my school friends were Jewish. We attended a Passover Seder and I was invited to Bar Mitzvah's in High School. Once someone asked me what religion I was and I responded, "Orthodox." To which they said, "Never heard of a Jew named Mills." I got that a lot in school. Having Jewish friends gave me a larger outlook on religion and life. Even though I was firmly rooted in my faith I was instilled with a deep sense of openness and understanding to those who were different from me, something that I try to maintain to this day. After all, Jesus was Jewish and what better education than to learn about the ancient faith Jesus came from?

CHAPTER 3

My Little Black Dress

After a lot of soul searching and speaking with Father Paul and Mom I decided to apply to seminary. I remember telling my college roommates that I had applied. It was fall 1993. Mike and Jeff were sitting at our small kitchen table in our campus apartment:

"Hey guys, not sure how to tell you, so I'll just come out and say it. . ."

"You're gay?" Jeff chortled.

"No, I'm not gay. I'm applying to seminary."

Jeff and Mike kept eating their sandwiches.

"Did you hear what I said? I'm going to seminary in the fall. It's in New York." I thought they hadn't heard me so I repeated myself.

Mike shoveled some potato chips into his mouth.

"Aren't you surprised?" I asked. I was expecting them to laugh or something.

"No."

"No?" I said.

"You've hinted about it during the year and we saw the course catalog sitting on your desk." Mike replied.

"Yep," Jeff interrupted between bites, "Not surprised. By the way, what do you do at seminary anyway, pray all day?"

"Kind of," I said.

"Like twice a week or something?"

"No, twice a day during most of the year, three times a day during Lent."

"Man, that's a lot of Church, once a week is enough for me. Ain't that right, Jeff?" Mike looked up at Jeff smiling.

"Don't ask me, I go twice a year, Christmas and Easter."

We all laughed and continued eating our sandwiches. I was relieved that my friends affirmed my decision. It wasn't easy sharing my future plans, especially since I wasn't aware of anyone in my class planning on going into seminary. One of the first things I needed to do was buy a cassock.

Many men are required to wear a shirt and tie to work, but as a seminarian and priest-in-training I was required to wear an ankle-length black dress. Not an off-the-rack either, but a custom-made, dry-clean-only one that would last at least three years if not more. I still have my original one. It hangs on the back of my office door. A few months ago I tried it on just to see if it still fit. It fits, but barely. I like to think it's because of all those dry cleanings.

My black dress, which is called a cassock, is a garment that seminarians wear to chapel and that priests and pastors wear underneath their Sunday vestments. Protestant pastors refer to it as their preaching gown. The word cassock comes from the Middle French word *casaque*, which means a long coat. Some historians think that the cassock was akin to the undergarment that the Roman citizens wore underneath their toga, very similar to a tunic. In previous centuries it wasn't uncommon for clergy to wear cassocks as their everyday wear. Over time ministers transitioned to shirts and collars while many Orthodox clergy still wear cassocks as their common clothes.

A well-trained eye can differentiate the cut and style of various cassocks. It's similar to differentiating a prom dress, from a cocktail dress, or evening gown. Orthodox cassocks are loose fitting, have two buttons near the collar and one near the waist, and are wide around the lower leg and ankles. Catholic cassocks are form fitting and have buttons running up and down the center front seam. Catholic clergy of higher rank have thirty-three red buttons along the front of the cassock signifying the age of Jesus when he died. Anglican cassocks have thirty-nine red buttons signifying the thirty-nine articles of faith of the English Reformation. Anglican bishops wear purple cassocks while the pope wears a white one. In traditional Orthodox countries like Greece, Bulgaria, Russia, and Ukraine, it's not uncommon to walk into a tailor's shop and buy a cassock off the rack. Here, you order a cassock from a special ecclesiastical tailor.

I met Bill while I was home on winter break during my senior year of college. Bill was the seminary intern at Holy Resurrection and we had lunch together a few times. When I told Bill that I was accepted into seminary he gave me the lowdown on seminary culture, which included information about cassocks. Ask any woman about clothing and they'll tell you, an off-the-rack dress from Macy's isn't the same as an off-the-rack at Talbot's. I was planning to spend at least three hundred dollars on a cassock and wanted to make sure I bought a good one. I wanted a Cadillac, not a Chevette. Bill gave me Leslie's number and address. I immediately called, made an appointment to see her later that week, and off I went.

As I was driving I kept thinking about all the life changes: I had graduated from college six weeks earlier with a Bachelor's degree in History, moved back home for the summer, and was waiting to enter seminary. The seminary sent me the acceptance letter with a reading list and course schedule: Church History, Liturgical Theology, Church Music, Christian Education, and Old Testament. These sounded different from the courses that I'd recently had in college: Biology, Sociology, World Literature, and Philosophy.

When I arrived in Danbury I turned off the interstate onto State Road 64 and kept driving. Here the highway was long gone and I was in the bucolic Connecticut countryside, gentle rolling hills with white cottages, and colonial homes with front yard gardens. Everything looked like it came right out of *Martha Stewart Living*. Later I realized why; Martha Stewart lived one town over. Some yards were overgrown with wild flowers, others had mounds of pink zinnias, purple and blue delphiniums, and black-eyed-Susans. Others had clumps of rambling red and white roses trailing along fence posts. Up ahead I saw Leslie's street and turned into the driveway. Her property was like the others, a longish meandering rock and pebble driveway with wildflowers in the front. The house was two stories, white, and had a screened front porch. I turned off the car, walked along the sidewalk and knocked on the door. Leslie answered. She wore baggy blue jeans and a comfy looking t-shirt. She had a round face and her salt and pepper hair was tied neatly in a bun with a simple hair clip. A few straggly pieces hung down the side. She looked like a middle-aged hippie.

"You didn't get lost driving here did you? *Everyone* seems to get lost once you get off the main road." Any minute I was waiting for her to say "peace," "groovy," or "dude."

"Come in, come in, excuse the mess on the porch." She stepped aside and led me past piles of old newspapers, magazines and towers of open boxes with knickknacks in them. There were boxes on the floor, boxes on tables, boxes on chairs and boxes atop of boxes. Someone could have died in here and been lost forever under those piles.

The house was cool and dark. The windows were open to a slight breeze, reminding me of childhood summers sleeping with the windows open. We stopped near the kitchen and entered a large open space,

"Well, this is my workshop, whaddya think?"

This was a seamstress's heaven. Bolts of tightly wound black material piled high, some dark black and others lighter shades of black. Another table was piled with bolts of beige, grey, and navy blue material, and yet another had bolts of gold, forest green, maroon, purple, red, and white. Next to these large piles were smaller piles of straggly scraps about the size of a large index card, some bigger and some smaller, and large clear yogurt-size plastic containers with buttons, tassels, and appliques with crosses on them.

"What a collection." I said.

"That's what happens when you're a seamstress. You keep *everything*."

"So Bill tells me you used to work on Broadway?"

"Well, more like off Broadway. I mended costumes. It was fun, but *very* tiring. But now I've turned to ecclesiastical attire." She seemed confident, and judging from the amount of work, she must have been well respected. Anyone who worked on Broadway for any length of time, even off Broadway, must be good.

"So, you're here for your first cassock?" Before I could answer, she continued, "But I hope not your last. First we have to pick material. I'm assuming black, right?"

Seminarians were required to wear black so that everyone looked the same, but after ordination you were allowed to wear other colors such as navy blue, grey, or beige. I really wanted a beige, but for now had to settle for black. Having everyone wear the same color cassock may seem innocuous, but this was just one example of conformity, very much like the military. Everyone wears the same uniform, everyone takes the same classes, everyone attends chapel and eats the same food. I didn't realize how much the formation process, even something as simple as one's attire, affected me. Over time one can easily lose one's autonomy and identity.

"As you see we have a wide variety of material. Over on this table we have some dupioni silk." It was shiny under the lights. She continued, "Now, just so you know, this is very expensive, but also long lasting." She handed me a sample. It felt very smooth between my fingers,

"When you say expensive, what are we talking about?"

"Oh, well, let's see, probably about six to seven hundred."

"I think I'll pass." I said, rolling my eyes. I would have loved to have one of those but I didn't have unlimited funds. I had champagne tastes, but a beer budget. I also had to purchase books, buy gas, and save spending money for food and incidentals.

I stood there staring at all the fabrics.

"Confusing, right?" She smiled. She must have read my mind.

"You can say that again. I thought it would be easy. I wasn't prepared for all of this."

"That's what most guys say. No off-the-rack here. This is all one-hundred-percent custom-made cassocks made by yours truly. Only the best. Let's measure you first and then we'll pick out the material after. Okay?"

"Sure."

She walked over to her sewing table and picked up a yellow measuring tape. "Okay, let's see. Stand facing me, shoulders back and eyes straight ahead. I want to measure your height first. The bottom of the cassock should be just above the top of your shoe so when you walk you won't trip, and when you need to climb the stairs you just pick it up around your waist."

She stood in front of me and with one hand put the top of the tape measure on my lower neck and measured to my belt buckle and wrote down the number on a piece of paper. Then she measured me from my belt buckle to the top of my ankle, just below my shin. I felt important, like a diplomat or a Wall Street banker. I never had a custom-made anything before let alone a black dress. This was a big deal.

"Now we're going to measure your chest and then your arms. Hold out your arms like you're flying a plane." She stood right in front of me and wrapped the tape measure around my chest and then went from my neck all the way to my wrist and wrote down some numbers.

"I build in a few extra inches just in case you gain those freshmen fifteen, but if you gain too much you're in trouble."

"You know, I was just going to ask about that."

"They all do, trust me. Problem is, if you gain too much, well, you'll be seeing me for a new cassock soon."

We both laughed.

"Well, I hope I won't be gaining too much."

"You better not. Some of these guys return after a few years and they're big as a house. All they do is eat, eat, and eat. Gotta put them on a diet." She was right. Over the years I met pastors who were very obese. Research shows that clergy are more overweight than the general population. There is food at every parish function. There is food at home, food at Church, food at people's homes, and food at conferences. After a while you just find yourself eating all the time. One day you'll wake up and you need a new pair of pants because the old ones don't fit anymore. Obesity contributes to other health problems: diabetes, increased blood pressure, extra stress on the knees and hips.

She stopped writing measurements and looked over at me.

"So which do you want? The tropical or the poly-wool blend?"

It didn't take long for me to decide,

"I think I'll take the poly-wool."

"Good choice. Let me grab my order form and write this down before I forget."

I stood there for a moment thinking that I had just made a big decision. I didn't know it then, but four years later I would return for two more cassocks and my first set of vestments.

"Okay, let's see, one poly-wool Russian style, that's three hundred plus twenty for shipping. I get half now and half on arrival. I'll send the cassock with a care card. Dry clean only, otherwise you'll ruin it."

Six weeks later a box arrived. I put the box on the kitchen table, opened it up, unwrapped the cassock, walked into the dining room and turned on the lights so I could look at myself in the mirror that Mom had above the sideboard. It felt awkward at first putting my arms in and finding the buttons and the hooks. When I looked up, there I was dressed in my new black dress which would be my uniform for the rest of my life. Ironically I never wanted to wear a uniform. My father wore a uniform to work and I didn't want to be like him.

Later that year, when I arrived on campus, all the guys wore their cassock to chapel. I fit right in and it didn't feel strange that I was wearing a long black dress. If I wore this on Madison Avenue people might stare, but on our little suburban campus I was fine.

I was surprised once when I showed up at a clergy gathering wearing a shirt and collar rather than a cassock. They are common in Eastern European countries like Bulgaria and Romania and even in the Middle East, but certainly not here in America. I couldn't imagine myself at the grocery store wearing an ankle-length black dress. I quickly learned my lesson and next time I showed up in a cassock. Once a priest told me that he and two other clergy were eating lunch at a local café wearing their cassocks, they didn't want to be confused with clergy from other denominations such as the Catholics or Anglicans. The waitress came over to the table and asked, "So which order are you guys from? Franciscan or Jesuit?"

Didn't Jesus tell his disciples to pray in secret and God the Father will reward you in secret? Didn't he warn his disciples specifically *not to* want the best seats and seek accolades and garner attention? So much for trying to be different.

Mom and Dad always taught me to practice the Christian faith in small acts of love and kindness, seeking not to bring attention to myself. Father Paul taught me that as Christians our job is not to convert the world, just love folks for who they are, wherever they are in life. Over the years he took me out to lunch and wore his clergy shirt and suit jacket. These guys at the restaurant were no better than the street preachers yelling and hollering about hellfire and brimstone. They think they are doing a good thing, but in the end they turn people off.

Then there was the incident in Dallas. It was our annual diocesan clergy convention. The parking lot was full and I had a hard time finding a parking spot. I walked into the hotel with my cassock swaying back and forth trying not to get it caught in the revolving door. As I checked in at the front lobby I heard clapping and women's voices coming from one of the banquet rooms. I thought nothing of it. Later I walked over to the elevator and pushed the up button and waited. The doors opened and before me, were three women dressed from head to toe in bright pink, staring at me in my black dress and big silver cross hanging down my chest. Looking closer I noticed their lapel buttons: "Mary Kay Convention 2003." So here we were, grown men in black dresses prancing about with women in pink pantsuits, blouses, and skirts. Talk about visual dissonance.

I still wear my cassock for Church services and my clericals for home visitations. During the week I wear regular street clothes or *civvies* as they're called. People should be drawn to us for the love, care, concern, and compassion that we offer quietly and in small ways, not for the clothes that we wear. My neighbors know that I'm a pastor and treat me like everyone else. I don't want to be treated differently because I wear a collar and I certainly don't want to start up a conversation or a staring contest because I'm walking along Main Street. Maybe I'm wrong? All I know is that my cassock hangs in the Altar where I'll put in on next Saturday night for services.

CHAPTER 4

Nirvana

I entered Saint Vladimir's Orthodox Theological Seminary in September 1994. The seminary is located on Scarsdale Road, a quaint tree-lined residential street in Crestwood, New York, a small section of streets and homes tucked away in Yonkers. Originally established in 1938, the seminary moved from its former location near Union Seminary in New York City to Crestwood in 1961. One could easily drive by and mistake it for a park, with its small brook flowing through the center of the grounds and a wall of pine trees along the street.

The seminary was named after Prince Vladimir, the leader of the Rus' tribes that inhabited the area around modern Ukraine and western Russia. The Rus', now known as the Russians, adopted Christianity in 988 AD. Two brothers, Cyril and Methodius, missionaries from modern day Macedonia, brought Orthodox Christianity to the Rus' peoples. They translated the Bible and the liturgy from Greek into local tribal languages and created a written alphabet called Cyrillic, after its creator, Cyril. History reports that Vladimir accepted Christianity freely, as did the rest of his kingdom, but the tales leave out the swords and death threats. In other words, Vladimir gave his people a choice, jump in the river and accept Jesus or die. I later found out that Vladimir was not alone, this happened all the time, kings or queens adopted Christianity and all their subjects became Christian too, no questions asked and if anyone ever said no, they would pay for it later. Christians tend to highlight all the wonderful things we've done in the world and somehow manage to gloss over our deep dark past.

I studied two-thousand years of theology: Church History, Liturgy, Old and New Testaments, ancient Greek, Liturgical Music, Bioethics, Christian Education, Pastoral Care, and Preaching. I had classes on Early Monasticism and The Priest as Liturgical Celebrant. In Church History we learned about the young Theodosia, who desired to live in a monastery, but because she was a woman, was forbidden to do so. So she took matters into her own hands and entered the monastery anyway, cutting her hair, wearing the monastic habit, and calling herself Theodore. Years later, at her death, her true identity was revealed when the monks removed her clothes to prepare her body for burial. Or the famous fifth-century writer and theologian, Origen of Alexandria, who was said to have taken Jesus' command in Matthew, "Some made themselves eunuchs for the kingdom," a bit too literally. I learned that there were more than four gospels and that Paul didn't write all the letters that have been attributed to him. We debated whether or not the Virgin had pain in childbirth. After all, if she was God's mother how could she have been in pain? Our female classmates *didn't* agree with that one bit. We learned about sinners who later became saints and saints who were sinners. Seminary isn't too different from law school or medical school, where the faculty force you to question and rethink what you know as they tear you down in order to build you up again. I tell my non-religious friends that seminary was like having a theological enema. My thoughts, ideas, and images of God and the Church were literally emptied, ripped apart, and reconfigured. Little did I know that this would soon happen again after I became a pastor.

We also read a lot. I mean *a lot*. My bookshelves are filled with books my neighbors haven't read: *The Erotic Word, Our Mother Saint Paul, Worship Traditions in Armenia and the Neighboring Christian East, Scripture and Tradition, The Battle for God,* and the *Nestle-Aland 4th Revised Edition of the Greek-English Bible.* Speaking of Bibles, I have them all nicely arranged on the shelf behind my desk: *The Jerome Bible, Revised Standard Version,* the *New Revised Standard Version,* the *New Revised Standard Ecumenical Study Version, Harper Collins Study Bible, King James Version, New King James Version, New International Version, The Message,* and *Today's Version for Common Man.* I entered seminary with one Bible, now I have twelve.

We read, we studied, and we took notes. My time was spent in three places: the classroom, the chapel, and in my bedroom where I stayed up past midnight working on term papers and projects. Life was like working the second shift at a factory: you work all night, come home and collapse.

I had no social life except for a night or two with friends enjoying a burger and a beer at the local pub. Otherwise my life was devoted to prayer and study.

The big problem was that this learning was done individually. *I* took notes, *I* read, and *I* wrote. There were no group projects or presentations. Yet in parish life I realized that most of ministry requires working with people: meetings, workdays, committees, and projects. I had to learn to work in small and large groups of people. At seminary we were taught to be theological experts. We had classes on Serbian Church History and classes on the ancient history of the Matins service, but how do they help with organizing a parish council or starting a pledge campaign? They don't. While we learned a lot, most of it didn't impact our future parish ministries.

I used to think books would teach me all that I needed to know to be a good pastor. I was wrong. I realized something was missing. I loved reading, studying, and writing, and even today could easily spend half a day browsing books in a bookstore. But all of this study, while important, is limited.

Eventually I gave away many of my academic books to seminary students from our parish. Over the years I have added more books to my growing collection; poetry, short stories, and memoirs. There is just as much theology in short stories by Anton Chekov, Lorrie Moore, and George Saunders as in academic tomes. I learned that one doesn't have to read about the Trinity to realize what community and communion are all about. Literature is a constant reminder that life is complicated, that all of us suffer in so many ways, and that the line between saint and sinner, good and bad, light and darkness, is more often than not very blurry. If I were revising a seminary curriculum I would certainly add a course on faith and fiction or a course on faith and film, exposing students to the intersection of Christianity and culture and how great literature and film can inspire our preaching and teaching.

Once Mom called me on the hall payphone,

"So Billy, what are you studying?"

"Oh, not much Ma, Greek verb declensions, Paul's use of *agape* in Romans, and the *homoousios* and *homoousion* debate. I have a paper due next week on the life of Saint. Barsanuphius and his brother Paphnutius. That's about it."

Dead silence.

"Ma, you there?"

"Yeah, I'm here."

She had no clue what I had said. She couldn't have cared less about Greek verb declensions or the *homoousios* debates. All she knew was that her son was devoted to ministry. All I cared about was that she kept sending tuition checks. Over the years she'd call and we'd have similar conversations. I tried my best to explain the ins and outs of Saint Gregory Nanzianzus' *Five Theological Orations on the Trinity* and Origen's *First Principles* but she didn't seem interested. She also didn't like it when I told her that Moses probably didn't exist and the Exodus story didn't happen exactly as it is in the Bible. Looking back, I don't blame her. She must have thought I was crazy. I thought I was smarter than her because I knew more about the Bible, about the Virgin Mary, about icons, and about the sacraments. I thought she was a simpleton because she lit her candles and kneeled at her pew reciting the Lord's Prayer, while I learned about the history of the Lord's Prayer and why we have pews. She had no idea about the Bible, but I studied the Bible inside and out. I went to seminary presumably to be a servant leader, but I was full of myself. Sure I knew more about the Church, but she knew much more about compassion and love than I ever did. She knew more about caring for the dying and the grieving than I ever learned in my course on death and dying. She changed diapers, wiped snot and saliva, emptied bedpans, and changed beds, and washed floors. What did I do all day? Wrote term papers and sang in the choir. I complained about lectures being too long and getting a bad grade on a test and she held the hand of dying patients. She knew more about patience and prayer and service than I did. She could have taught me about God and ministry if I had just taken the time to listen. I was so self absorbed in my little theological world that I lost touch with the one person who set me on this path in the first place.

It was much later that I realized that there was a disconnect between seminary studies and people in the pew. I didn't know that most people just want to be reminded that God loves them, that life is hard, and it's okay to fail and fall. It took me a long time to realize that most people weren't interested in the details of the fifth ecumenical council or the nuances of early Russian Church History; they just wanted their pastor to listen and love them, not judge them. They wanted to feel connected to Christ and to the community of faith. While I had a stellar theological education, I didn't have classes in psychology or human development. I didn't have training in leading or organizing groups or how to work with committees.

I couldn't read a parish budget, nor did I have a clue how to start a Church School program. I never saw the inside of a prison, nursing home, health clinic, or homeless shelter until I was in the parish. We had no experience with people with disabilities, or immigrants, or the homeless. We lived in proximity to New York City, an urban paradise for ministry, but we had no exposure to any of it. I was ill-equipped equipped for parish ministry. I had to learn the hard way, which almost sent me packing.

After lunch I usually took a brisk walk. Walking helped me unwind and get my mind off classes. While walking along those peaceful streets I wondered what our neighbors were doing. What was their life like? I often saw people walking to the train station and young moms pushing strollers. They were leading ordinary lives. On campus we walked around in our black dresses while these people worked hard, trying to make a good life for their children and grandchildren. I'd walk those streets dreaming about what type of parish I'd have and who my parishioners would be. These people were worried about making sure they had enough money in their retirement fund or whether or not they'd have enough tuition money for college. We were living in our ecclesiastical bubble, unaffected by the real life that was taking place around us.

You might be asking yourself how it is that a college graduate would devote six years to learning the basic theological foundations of Christianity and preparing for the priesthood. As I pointed out earlier, if you're wondering whether I had one of those Hollywood moments when the heavens open and God spoke to me, I didn't. It never happened. No Hollywood moments, no angelic visitations, no apparitions of the Virgin Mary, no burning bush, and no bolts of lightning. My entire life was a preparation for ministry. I had a loving and caring priest who took a genuine interest in my life. I'm sure if Father Paul had a different personality or hadn't been interested in me, I probably wouldn't have entered ministry. My regular participation in Church school, youth group activities, summer Church camp, and winter break retreats all helped form and shape me into who I was to become. All of these people and experiences went into the soup pot of life, simmered for years, and eventually turned out a pastor. So I guess Mom was right when she said, "One day you'll thank me for this." It's likely that if I hadn't been an Altar server or hadn't attended summer Church camp, I might not have gone into ministry. If we hadn't attended so many services I wouldn't have been exposed to the fullness of Church life, the songs, the sacraments, and the saints.

Full time seminary students had volunteer work, whether answering phones, cleaning hallways, helping in the kitchen, sorting mail, cutting grass, or shelving books in the library. For two years I served as the lunch crew captain. It wasn't a job that I would have chosen. The Dean of Students assigned the community service jobs and unless you had some serious health issues you had to fulfill your job assignment. Later I learned that parish ministry was like that. There were plenty of things that I didn't want to do but had to whether I liked it or not. How many moms want to wake up at two o'clock in the morning and change diapers? How many wives want to take care of their terminally ill husbands? How many dads want to work an extra part time job in order to pay for college tuition? People do what they have to do.

Every day at one o'clock the four-member lunch crew ran down to the refectory and served lunch. We set the tables, put out the food, and then afterwards cleaned up and washed dishes. It was hard work. The washroom was especially difficult because the dishwasher spewed steam and you left the lunchroom sweaty and damp. I often had to change my shirt for my afternoon class.

The one job that no one wanted, the job that everyone dreaded, was sacristan. The sacristan was responsible for arriving early for chapel, lighting all the candles, bringing up the vestments from the basement, ringing the bells, and making sure there was enough wine, bread, charcoal, and incense.

On the first day of school, I checked my mailbox and found a plain white envelope with my name on it. I quickly opened the letter. Inside was a short typed letter from the Dean of Students: William Mills, Sacristan. Didn't they know that I was a third year student and I wanted an easy job? Didn't they know that I had books to read and papers to write?

I made an appointment with Father Paul Lazor the Dean of Students. He was intimidating to say the least, dressed all in black sitting in his leather chair behind his desk. After I took a seat in his office and before I got a word out he said, "You know Bill, I am so glad that you're going to be the sacristan this year. You are such a dedicated student, responsible, caring, and kind." Of course he said it with a smile and I was flattered. He had this charming way of talking with you, like he knew what you were going to say before you said it. After hearing all of those compliments how could I argue with him? No one argued with Father Paul. I thanked him and walked out of the office, knowing that there was no way I could get out of the sacristy job that year.

This was a problem for me and people like me, who were people pleasers. It was hard to say no to those who had authority over you and your future. He was a priest. He was a professor. He was a gatekeeper. If you said no to one of his requests he may or may not put in a good word for you in the faculty senate when your name came up for ordination review. He may or may not write a recommendation letter for you. Seminary administrators had a lot of spiritual and emotional authority over us. So you'd say yes. Yes to the sacristy job and yes to a gazillion volunteer opportunities. Yes to teaching a night class for the professor because he is sick. This means that you lose sleep, and less sleep means that you're constantly irritable and angry. Resentment builds up. You don't learn to take care of yourself. You don't eat right. You want to exercise but you can't because you're tired. Your life becomes one job after another. You have no life. You begin to lose your humanity. All your professors who are pastors tell you that you are called to be servants. You keep saying yes, until one day you come home and collapse, you wonder who you are and what you've become. I don't think this is what Jesus had in mind when he called his apostles; called to serve, called to listen, called to love, called to forgive, but you give and give and give and you give more until you're empty. Unfortunately it's years later that you eventually learn to say no and take back some control over your life, but then it's almost too late. The damage has been done.

During my third year I had a recurring nightmare. My nightmare was that I overslept and jumped out of bed, ran to chapel, and when I walked in, the entire seminary community was already there and was laughing at me. I would look down and see that I was still in my pajamas. I had that dream a lot.

Seminary was a lot like the military. Our days revolved around chapel, study, and completing our work assignments. We had very little free time. Matins followed by breakfast. Classes were taught in two-hour blocks from nine o'clock until one, when we had lunch. We had twenty minutes to eat and then the lunch crew had twenty minutes to clean up. Free time was spent taking walks, napping, exercising, or using the library and working on research papers. After our evening classes we studied, watched the television in the rec room, or commiserated about classes, relationships, or professors. During Lent we had another service at nine o'clock called Compline, which was conducted by candlelight. It lasted about twenty-five minutes, but by the end of the day we were exhausted. You went to bed and woke up again the next day and did it all over again.

The food was different from what I was used to. In college it was mostly meat and potatoes, vegetables, and fruit. There was an ice cream bar, salad bar, sandwich bar, and pizza station. I'll never forget the day, sometime during Lent, when I looked down and saw a large white serving bowl filled with black beans soaking in a thick layer of olive oil. I asked one of my fellow students what it was and he said, "Jackie's famous black bean soup. You better get used to it, we have it a lot during Lent." And he was right. We had that soup at least twice a week. I managed to eat most of the corn bread that she served with it. If I don't eat another black bean, it's fine by me.

Jackie was out of place on our all-white campus. A short, thin, chain-smoking African American lady from the Bronx, Jackie was in her early 60s and occasionally cussed, too, "Don't you smell my damn food! It's good! During Lent she'd say, "I know you guys go over to Taco Bell and have yourselves those beef burritos, I see your cars over there." She was right, we were tired of eating beans and rice during those long Lenten days.

After dinner she'd slowly make her way to her car, carrying her pocketbook and some leftovers. I always wondered what Jackie thought of us, a bunch of single, middle-class kids studying obscure liturgical texts and debating how Jesus was both human and divine, while she stood in that hot kitchen all day cutting and dicing onions and tomatoes and whipping up her famous pies and cakes. Judging from her age and the look on her face and hands she knew more about hard work than we ever would. She knew about money and paying bills and service and hospitality. She knew about serving her neighbor. She also knew about suffering and hardship. While Jackie couldn't conjugate a Greek verb or exegete a passage from Mark's Gospel, she knew about work and the world, about faith and life. I watched her cracked hands chop and dice carrots or stir a large vat of bean chili over her six-burner stove.

Even though it was 1994, it felt more like 1954. It was a culture shock leaving college where I shared an apartment with four friends, had my own television, a full kitchen, and my own schedule. One of my friends requested to have a personal phone hooked up in his bedroom so he could access his email account. The administration said *no*. The reason? Students were not allowed to have personal phones in the room. Another friend of mine wanted to work part time because he was paying for seminary himself. The administration said no. Case closed.

Looking back this all sounds silly, the emphasis on rules, regulations, and authority. I could see how some students were attracted to the rules and regulations and eventually adopted these qualities into their own pastoral ministries. It was about authority, power, and control.

We had a calling to serve God and his Church. We were being prepared for big and great things. We were part of the grand institution called the Church, with a rich and colorful two-thousand-year history, a history with popes, bishops, priests, monasteries, and seminaries. We were preparing to go out into the big wide world and preach the Gospel. We were going to build big buildings and awe our flocks with our pastoral skills. We were a band of brothers; all for one and one for all. We were different from everyone else and we knew it. We had degrees. We were educated. We were Masters of Divinity. Jesus told his disciples that he came to usher in his kingdom, and the gates of hell would not prevail against it. We took that to heart. Some guys wanted to serve as military chaplains and pray with troops, others wanted to be hospital chaplains, some went into academia, and guys like me wanted to be parish priests.

The high point of my seminary career was ordination to the priesthood. Ordination is akin to being commissioned as an officer in the Army. The word *ordination* comes from the Latin word *ordinatio*. In Christian theology *ordination* means a setting aside in the community of faith. In the Scriptures people have always been set aside or appointed for leadership positions: Moses and Aaron, Jeremiah and Jonah, Paul and Timothy, and Prisca and Acquilla. My ordination day would be the culmination of my seminary studies. I had no idea how strange that day would be.

CHAPTER 5

Ordination Day Nightmare

Ordination day finally arrived: Saturday, November 13, 1999, the Feast of Saint John Chrysostom. John's surname comes from the Greek meaning "the golden-mouthed," although he should be remembered as a big mouth. A fourth-century pastor and Archbishop of Constantinople, John was a powerful preacher, proclaiming the Gospel to a largely pagan population. He cared for the poor and the widows, and supported his fellow pastors. His bold preaching put him in direct conflict with the Empress Eudoxia, to whom he referred on several occasions as the whore of Babylon. John was certainly an able pastor but not a great diplomat. Eudoxia didn't take kindly to his comments and exiled him three times, the last time to Armenia, where he died in 407. John, together with his friends, Basil the Great and Gregory the Theologian, are considered the three shining lights of theology and the seminary chapel is named after them: Three Hierarchs Chapel.

My life had led up to this day: ten years of Sunday school, twelve years of summer Church camp, four years of college, and six years of seminary. It was all over. Ordination day was everything. It also meant that in a few months I'd be assigned to a parish, and, like John, put in conflict with parishioners who wanted to exile me from the parish.

It's nine o'clock and the two seminary choirs begin singing as we await the bishop's grand entrance. Waiting for the bishop's entrance is like waiting for the bride at a wedding; you wait, and wait, and wait some more until he finally arrives. I was nervous, but I was ready.

I stand in the middle of the chapel with two other deacons under the large domed ceiling and glass windows where the soft autumn sun shines down and reflects off our gold vestments. We swing silver-plated censers back and forth like children swinging yo-yos up and down while little white puffs of smoke ascend heavenward.

My mom stands in front, near the Altar, in her maroon dress with black shoes, camera in hand and ready to take pictures. Her hair is in a perm. She is clearly a proud mother. This is her son's ordination. It's a bittersweet occasion for both of us knowing that my father couldn't be here, Having died of a heart attack a decade earlier. Little did she know that she would be dead in four years, the result of a lengthy battle with liver disease.

Today I stand where hundreds of young men like me once stood, awaiting the entrance of their ordaining bishop, looking forward to their ordination and awaiting their parish assignment. Standing in the middle of it all, I realize that I'm just one person in a long line of men who have been called to serve God and His Church.

I'm also anxious. Three days before my ordination, a friend, Mary Ellen, who had promised to prepare and cook a luncheon for me, had a stroke. Thankfully she survived but was hospitalized. We were now on Plan B, which meant we had to prepare and cook a meal for around a hundred guests. In a last minute frenzy we did all the shopping, arranging and setting of tables, and food preparation. The night before my ordination we set out the flowers, baked several dozen blueberry muffins, and prepared the egg and sausage casseroles. I was worried that there wouldn't be enough food for our guests. However, more than anything, I was worried about Mary Ellen.

As the choir finishes their last hymn, the moment comes. Two seminarians dressed in black cassocks push open the doors while another seminarian begins ringing the bronze bells signaling the entrance of Bishop Peter L'Huillier. He stumbles in, grabbing the arms of one of the seminarians. His longtime diabetes has robbed him of several toes and he is a bit wobbly. David, his driver and personal valet had arrived a few minutes earlier and placed a glass of orange juice and insulin in the sacristy area just in case Bishop Peter needed it during the service. Bishop Peter wears a tall stove-pipe hat with a black satin veil that rests gently on his shoulders and flows mid-way down his back: which is the common dress of a monk. Two seminarians escort him into the chapel, one holding the long fringes of his port-wine-colored cape that drags several feet on the floor, while the other carries his silver-topped crozier, which looks like a shepherd's crook, an ancient sign of his episcopal authority. Bishop Peter is French and although he's been living in the United States for over twenty years, he talks like Inspector Clouseau of the *Pink Panther* movies. "Allo Fazzer Villiams, good to zee you," he would say in his high-pitched voice. Not only is he a ruling bishop he is also a professor of Canon Law, an area of theology concerning the ancient rules and regulations of Church life. Like a typical professor he'd go off on thirty-minute tangents; one minute you'd be in the third century, studying why men with one testicle can't serve at the Altar and the next minute he'd start talking about the fineries of a good Bordeaux or Chardonnay.

I'm now standing at the right side of the Altar table, about a foot away from the sacristy room, a small room off the side of the altar where we keep the vestments, wine, candles, and incense. I'm waiting my turn to go out for my series of petitions. The choir is pitch perfect as usual. The four-part *a capella* choir sings as one voice offering up their prayer and praise to God.

The service goes along fine until I feel a hard tug on my right shoulder. My head whips around, "Go over and get Bishop Peter's prayer book. Now," David barks. David is short and stocky with a crew cut. Every week he'd drive Bishop Peter to campus, assist him to the classroom, and then hang out in the main building. He often wore a white t-shirt with blue overalls and looked like he could have been one of the members of the *The Village People*.

"What?" I say.

"Go over and get the bishop's book, now," David enunciates each word like a schoolteacher, his grip tightening on my right arm. I stare at him. This is supposed to be a peaceful day. It wasn't turning out that way.

"Leave me alone," I say turning my head.

Andrew, a third year student, medium build with wide shoulders, comes up behind David and says, "Let go of him now."

All the while the service continues. The deacon chants his petitions and the choir responds, "Lord have mercy." In the Altar, David, Andrew, and I are having a shoving match.

"I *said* get off of him," Andrew says as he grabs David by his shoulders and shoves him against the counter, pinning him against the sink. One of the priests looks over in our direction. David shoots Andrew a stern look. I don't know what's going on. We're at a Liturgy and here in the Altar is a wrestling match.

Andrew grabs David with both hands and escorts him outside.

"Don't come back until later," Andrew says.

And with that he shuts the sacristy door and locks it.

It's now time for the ordination proper. Two deacons lead me to the center of the chapel facing the Altar. There's no turning back. It's like standing at the Altar waiting for your bride to come, it's now or never. They both shout in unison the word, *Command,* and I fall to my knees, making a full prostration to the ground, with my head touching the floor. We stand again and then they lead me a few feet forward and shout, *Command.* I go to my knees again and make a full prostration on the ground. Finally they lead me through the center Altar doors shouting, *Command,* as I enter and make a full prostration at the front of the Altar table. As the choir sings, I'm led around the altar three times. Each time I go around, the choir sings:

> *O holy martyrs who fought the good fight and have received your crowns, entreat ye the Lord that our souls may be saved.*
>
> *Glory to thee, O Christ God, the Apostles boast, the martyrs joy, whose preaching was the consubstantial Trinity.*
>
> *Rejoice O Isaiah! A Virgin is with child, and shall bear a Son Emmanuel both God and man, and Orient is his name; whom magnifying we call the Virgin blessed.*

After the third time around I kneel at the right corner of the table, my head resting on my folded hands. Bishop Peter places his hands on my head and reads the ancient prayers aloud, "*The grace divine that heals that which is infirm and completes that which is lacking elevates through the laying-on of hands William Christopher the most devout deacon to be a Priest. Wherefore let us pray for him, that the grace of the Holy Spirit may come upon him.*"

Yes, divine grace is what I need. The more the better. During our studies we heard about sin and salvation, hope and despair. We sat at our desks dreaming big dreams about our future parishes and the people in them. We thought we knew what to expect. Little did we know.

After reciting another prayer, the ordination is over. Bishop Peter takes my left arm, raises me up, and leads me to the center of the Altar and presents me to the congregation. Friends and family are proud and I am grateful. This is for real. No longer a dream, a fantasy, I'm no longer just Bill, but *Father Bill.* Cameras start flashing. I feel like an actor in a photo shoot.

Bishop Peter exclaims, *Axios,* which is a Greek word meaning *worthy,* and the congregation responds loudly, *Axios,* and then the choir sings three times, *Axios, Axios, Axios.* At this solemn moment part of me wants to laugh: ordained on the feast of an exiled bishop, ordained by a bishop with missing toes, and a wrestling match in the Altar. It's all so bizarre. Obviously this isn't what I had in mind for my ordination day. Life is messy and things often don't go as planned. I certainly couldn't have planned this. I maintain composure as Bishop Peter vests me in gold vestments. He finally presents me with a silver cross inscribed with the words from 1 Timothy 4:12, "Let no one despise your youth, but set the believers an example in speech and conduct, in love, in faith, in purity." I'm twenty-seven and I'm a Father. Yet I don't feel like a Father, let alone an example to anyone. Bishop Peter called me worthy, yet I don't feel worthy. I don't feel worthy to preach sermons or hear confessions. I don't feel worthy to lead services. I never changed a diaper, paid a mortgage, or had a real job. How can I offer pastoral advice? I went straight from high school to college to seminary to ordination. I know that I have the approval of the Holy Synod of Bishops, the seminary faculty, my friends, and my family. Yet deep down I am terrified. Little do I know what awaits me in the parish.

CHAPTER 6

Meeting the Bishop

Parish assignments are mysterious. Every denomination does things differently. In the Orthodox Church parish assignments are a delicate dance between the bishop, the parish, and the priest. The bishop takes into consideration the specific gifts and talents of a pastor and tries to match up a pastor with a parish. This doesn't always work, but more often than not it does. If a pastor wants to serve in an inner city parish the bishop will look at this closely. Some priests want to start new missions and others prefer suburbia. There's no one-size-fits all when it comes to parish assignments.

Taisia and I had none of those concerns. Our only concern was that we would have a parish somewhere on the East Coast within a day's drive of New Jersey or Florida, close to our families. She was planning on being an art teacher and we thought she could get a job wherever that may be. So, with that in mind, we were off for our meeting with the bishop.

She and I first met while I was the summer intern at her father's parish in Longwood, Florida. Her father was the pastor and my primary task would be to shadow him as he went about his daily activities, similar to medical students shadowing residents. I helped organize summer church school, assisted with summer Church camp, sang in the choir, delivered sermons, and taught a weekly adult education class. While I was helping her dad, Taisia was finishing up her Bachelors degree.

We were invited to the Church headquarters at Oyster Bay Cove, a small bedroom community in eastern Long Island. Along the way I kept wondering how the meeting would go? I wondered about our options?

Everything was top secret, we knew we were having a meeting and that the bishop would have some choices for us, but we had no idea where these places were. Everything was so Byzantine. Even though it was the twentieth century it felt like the twelfth century. The Church still made decisions behind closed doors, word of mouth was powerful, and the more gatekeepers you knew the better. It was unnerving knowing that your future would be decided within a few hours. Thankfully neither of us was afraid of meeting the bishop or his chancellor. We had met them several times over the years on various occasions and were comfortable in their presence.

We pulled into the long tree-lined driveway at the Church headquarters. In front of us stood a crème colored 19th century Georgian revival-style house that was a mini version of the mansions one would see in Newport, Rhode Island or in rural Virginia. This place screamed money, power, and prestige. All they needed was a gate and a guard and you'd think you were at some executives' house.

The receptionist opened the door and told us that Father Bob and Metropolitan Theodosius, the head bishop of our Church, were out for dinner and would be back shortly. She showed us to his office.

She opened the door and invited us in. The office had large picture windows overlooking a garden, a desk and a sitting area with two leather club chairs, a sofa and coffee table. On the walls hung several icons of saints and pictures of visiting dignitaries. We waited a few minutes and then heard approaching footsteps. Father Bob and the Metropolitan walked in and we got up out of our chairs to greet them,

"Well, it's so good to see you two, so good. How are you?" Father Bob said as he and the Metropolitan walked in and motioned us to sit down. Father Bob was short with jet-black hair, probably colored, a little plump but not fat. The Metropolitan was also short but slimmer, a bit older than Father Bob, with salt-and-pepper hair and a neatly trimmed beard.

After small talk about the weather and the traffic and my seminary studies, we began our conversation.

"Father Bill, let me tell you. I have three options for your parish assignment, three very good options, or opportunities. I'm sure you want to hear about them, right?"

"Sure, go ahead," I said with some trepidation in my voice.

"All right, let's see, let's see." He walked over a few steps to his desk, reached for a piece of paper, and then sat back down. "First let me begin by telling you this meeting is just an informational meeting, nothing official yet. Ok? Just wanted to get that out in the open. We'll let you guys mull it over a while before we officially assign you somewhere."

That was good to hear. While I was tense I felt at ease knowing that we'd leave with some options but nothing formal.

"Sound good?" he asked.

We both nodded.

"Okay. First we have Holy Spirit Parish in Pennsylvania. Now I need to warn you it's a well-established parish, started in the late twenties, I think." He paused for a moment and then continued, "the salary isn't optimal . . ."

Well-established? In clergy talk well-established meant old, as in really old. As in the basement had mold, the dome leaked, and the average age was seventy. Basically he was telling me the place was a funeral factory. We heard plenty of similar stories in seminary. The Church is a small world and word travels fast, really fast. Former students would visit and tell us about congregational life. Holy Spirit parish probably needed more of the Holy Spirit if it was going to survive. It was most likely a few funerals short of closing. He must have seen my reaction because he quickly followed it up with talk about parish housing,

"I'm not sure exactly how much they pay, however the good news is. . ." My ears perked up when he said *good news*, "They have a gorgeous, really gorgeous, four-bedroom brick rectory. Just imagine, you don't have to worry about the extra car you can just walk to work."

Walk to work? No thanks. I'm all for getting exercise but didn't want to live above the store. I gave Taisia a quick glance and knew what she was thinking without saying anything. We had previously talked about our wanting to own our house. Both of our parents owned their homes and we wanted to do that too. Although a four-bedroom brick home sounded tempting I also realized that I'd pay in other ways. As Mom always said there's no such thing as a free lunch. Parish owned housing means that members dictate what type of decorations the clergy family can use or whether or not they can paint the interior or exterior. Then there's the problem of lost equity. When you retire you must vacate the rectory. All you have is your pension and hopefully some savings to rent or buy a small house or condo. Pastors who own their own house are much better off in the long run.

"Actually, we'd rather not live in parish-owned housing," I said.

The Metropolitan raised his eyebrows as if he were surprised.

"Why not?" Father Bob asked.

"Quite frankly, we want to own our own house and we don't want to lose out on the equity." I'm sure this sounded like we were bucking the system.

"That will certainly limit your options here in the Northeast you know, most parishes provide housing . . ."

In clergy-speak this translates as the parish pays the priest next to nothing. Sure, they pay the priest twenty-five thousand plus the right to live in a rectory. I knew one parish who promised their new priest a rectory but couldn't pay much of a salary so they gave him cases of tomatoes and cucumbers in lieu of payment. No thank you. I'd rather have fifty thousand and no rectory, although I wouldn't mind the cucumbers and tomatoes.

He continued, "There's another parish along the Thruway, from what I gather it's a bit of a challenge. . .."

Along the Thruway was once a booming area now gone bust. Large companies that were once the economic backbone had moved out long ago. The once busy and bustling Main Streets were mostly empty with foreclosed homes, business space for lease, and few jobs.

He also said *challenging*, which meant they were a bunch of trouble-makers. In seminary we had heard of parishes that devoured priests. The parish history read like a series of bad pitchers on the roster, one pastor stayed three years, another two, and one lasted six months. Pastors were berated by the parish council or paychecks withheld. No way was I going to raise a family in that situation. I was young, but I had enough common sense to refuse. Taking my chances I asked, "Is there anything else?"

"Well, there is one, but it's very small, not sure if you'll like it. It'll be available in June. The Nativity of the Theotokos, in Charlotte. Are you familiar with it?"

"A little bit."

I had heard from my father-in-law that Father Hank was planning to retire soon. He thought that the geographic location plus the smaller size of the parish would be good for me. I had no deep interest in heading South but if that was the only viable parish at the moment I would have to go.

Father Bob continued, "I only met the priest once, but they're not offering much salary and no rectory either. It's technically still a mission."

"That's okay. Right?" I looked over to Taisia. She nodded in agreement.

"Well, it's your decision. Missions don't always work out."

"Well we could always try," Taisia interjected.

North Carolina. I lived my entire life in the Northeast. I assumed North Carolina would be very different from the Northeast but it was a chance I had to take. The other two options weren't appealing and being a young couple we had to think ahead about good schools and neighborhoods for children. I certainly didn't want to be the pastor of a well-established, challenging, dying parish even if it had a gorgeous four-bedroom brick rectory. Of course money was an issue but both of us were industrious and we'd make things work.

"So it sounds like you guys are interested in Nativity, huh?"

"I think so."

"My advice would be for you to go visit before you commit to anything. When you return give me a call and we can talk. You can contact me after the holidays."

After the meeting Taisia and I walked out into the autumn evening. I showed Taisia into the car and got in. We were now officially closer to a new home.

CHAPTER 7

My First Date

It was the first week of December 1999. I was about to go on my first date. Not just any date, but a date with a future parish. It's not uncommon to visit with several parishes before being assigned to one. It's like speed dating, a weekend visit, a series of question and answer sessions, a dinner or two, and then off to another city and another parish. This date had to work out. It was this or nothing.

Three days before the trip I woke up with a runny nose, nothing major, just a case of the sniffles. The next day I had a sore throat and by day three I had all the symptoms of a full-blown winter cold: sneezing, watery eyes, a sinus headache, and to top it off, I lost my voice. Laryngitis is to a priest what bunions are to a dancer. I went through a bottle of Nyquil and a package of throat lozenges. How was I going to answer questions? How was I going to preach? I sounded like Kermit the Frog. I would have preferred staying home under the covers. My plane ticket was purchased and hotel room was booked. I had to go, cold or no cold. When I planned the trip the contact person told me that Walter and Linda would pick me up.

Walter was somewhere in his late fifties with a growing paunch, slicked back silver hair slowly creeping northwards. Linda was slightly younger than Walter with colored, reddish brown hair and wearing blue jeans that were a bit too tight for her age.

They suggested that we make a quick tour of Charlotte and then stop in to see the parish. It was late afternoon and the winter sun was low on the horizon. Walter graciously placed my bag in the trunk and I got into the back seat. The airport was quiet, only a handful of cars and a passing bus or two; very different from LaGuardia, with taxis buzzing around and the constant construction noise and car exhaust. Here the air was crisp and cool, not freezing like in New York, but cold enough for a light jacket or heavy sweater. I could get used to this. The sky was also different from New York. December in New York meant cloudy with a regular chance of freezing rain or light snow or both, a far cry from the blue sky I later found out was a hallmark of the Piedmont region of North Carolina. It was exciting being in a new city, but the big question was: would I like it? My idea of the South was what I learned from watching the *Dukes of Hazzard*; everyone had a sofa in the garage and a dog under the front porch. People drank moonshine, watched NASCAR, and ate biscuits and gravy. If we were going to live here we would have to accept a lot of new things. Would we be up to the task?

Off we went on our tour. Walter and Linda made small talk, asking about the plane ride, the weather, classes, the cost of gas and food, the usual ho-hum small conversation on a first date, nothing serious and nothing memorable either. Just the basic get-to-know you questions. Every so often I had to blow my nose or wipe my eyes; this cold was getting worse. I wanted to make a good impression, but it's hard when you have snot dripping from your nose. Walter took an off ramp and entered downtown. Linda pointed out some highlights,

"Father, straight ahead of us is Panther Stadium; do you like football?"

"No, I'm not a big sports fan," I said looking at the tall towers of glass. Truth was that I hated football. Why would three hundred pound grown men run around a field trying to get a small brown ball? My father loved football. On Sundays after Church he would watch NFL games all afternoon.

"Walter and I are big fans. Aren't we, Walter?"

Walter nodded in agreement, "Uh huh. Panthers going all the way this year."

"There it is over there," Linda pointed at the stadium up ahead.

After passing the stadium we kept on driving. Walter stopped at a red light and on my right I saw a large stucco building with a blue neon sign: "UPTOWN CABERET."

Walter caught my eye in the rear view mirror, "We have more strip clubs than Churches, don't we Linda?" He smiled looking over in her direction.

"Walter!" Linda's head whipped to her left,

"What? It's true," He said.

I felt like a teenager watching an R-rated movie with my parents. I wanted someone to change the conversation and fast.

"By the way, how do you pronounce your wife's name? I saw in the email that her name is spelled T-a-i-s-i-a." Linda annunciated each letter aloud like a first grade teacher,

"It's pronounced like *Thai* food and *s-y-a* at the end; it's an old Russian name," I said.

"Oh, I thought it was Tasha," Linda said.

"No, it's T-a-i-s-i-a," I repeated. Now *I* sounded like a first grade teacher.

She paused for a moment, "Tashishia?"

"No. Just T-a-i-s-i-a." I repeated each letter again. After a few times she still didn't get it.

We drove along a four-lane road with railroad tracks to our left and a string of warehouses. I couldn't see much in the dark, just a used car place, and a few lots for sale. Walter said that the Church was up ahead on the left.

He turned left into the gravel driveway, the headlights rested on the white painted sign in the front yard: *"Nativity of the Holy Theotokos Orthodox Church Sunday, Divine Liturgy 9:30 am."* The paint was peeling as if it had been standing there for a long time. Walter parked near the front door. I got out of the car and stretched my legs. The building was a rectangle, the size of two or three double-wide trailers pushed together, with beige aluminum siding, rust-colored doors and square windows. Passing drivers could easily mistake it for an office building. I quickly surveyed the property, no steeple, no dome, no bell tower, no fellowship hall, no rectory, no manicured lawn, just an aluminum box plopped in the middle of a field. I didn't expect Saint Patrick's Cathedral, but I didn't expect this either. Walking to the right side of the building I noticed roofing shingles piled about three high making a semi circle around the sides,

"What are those for?" I said pointing to the ground.

"Oh that. It's a makeshift sidewalk," Walter said. He looked at me for a reaction. I just stood there looking at the shingles on the ground wondering why they didn't use concrete.

While Walter and I made our way to the front, Linda unlocked the building. She led me into the fellowship area. In front were a few brown office tables with chairs on either side. To my right there was a large restaurant-style kitchen. The walls were white but turning taupe, signs of aging I guessed. The place looked like it needed a facelift, if not a total makeover.

Linda motioned me to follow, so I did. She walked a few paces ahead motioning me forward. Scattered about the blue linoleum floor were four medium-sized faux Persian rugs. There were a few rows of office-grade grey plastic chairs lined up. The rest of the sanctuary was open, which is typical in Orthodox Churches. I looked up, surveying the drop ceiling with fluorescent lighting. This certainly wasn't the Sistine Chapel.

I stood there taking everything in. Linda stood behind me quietly. I walked a little further and opened one of the doors that led into the Altar: a blast of neon blue paint that looked just like the UPTOWN CABERET sign. I quickly closed the door and took a few steps back and stood with Walter and Linda,

"So what do you think Father, you like it?" Linda asked.

"Interesting," I said. It was all that I could muster. What else *could I* say? I was expecting something a little more substantial, something that said *presence and permanence*. This said *work in progress*. Deep down I was hoping that it would be like Holy Resurrection, not fancy, but not a warehouse. I stood there realizing that this would be my new home for the foreseeable future. I was tired and asked Walter and Linda to drive me to my hotel.

The next day they picked me up for the dinner meeting. I was still nursing a cold and guzzling down cough medicine. I tried to keep hydrated which meant I had to keep running to the bathroom.

I walked into the fellowship area and saw that the parish council members, about seven of them, were already gathered, mingling about in the kitchen and in the hall. If my trip was my first date then this was a get-to-know-the-in-laws dinner. They had prepared a potluck supper in my honor. Walter introduced me to the parish council members and we started the buffet line. There were the usual Church potluck options of casseroles, soft dinner rolls, bean salad, vegetables and dip, plenty of chips and pretzels, and for dessert, some fruit pies. We sat around two large tables that were pushed together to make a large square. They saved a seat for me at the head of the table,

"Father, is this your first trip South?" Someone inquired.

"Yes and no. Mom and dad took me to Disney a few times in the summer, but that's about it, we never ventured much off I-95. Never been to this part of the state."

"How did you like your tour of Charlotte? Nice city huh?" someone else asked.

I wanted to say that I liked UPTOWN CABERET but this wasn't the time or place for that kind of humor.

"Lots of business, industry, I was impressed."

Someone else said, "Yep, both First Union and Lowe's have their headquarters in the area. Good for the economy and good for Charlotte."

I felt uncomfortable being peppered with questions. I felt like I was at a presidential press conference and everyone wanted to get their question answered. Since I wasn't on my A-game it was hard, but I also didn't have a lot of answers either. This was all new for me. I was wondering what they were thinking.

"Father, do you have plans, you know, for our parish?" Someone inquired.

"Plans?" I said as I took another bite of casserole. The only plan I had was to go back to the hotel and sleep. I wasn't prepared to answer big questions like this. I didn't know what to say. I came down here just to take things in. I didn't have any grand plans, not for myself, and certainly not for them.

"Can you grow our Church? You know, increase membership? We want to expand."

Before they could grow they had to take care of the place. It was in pretty bad shape and needed some tender loving care. I was in a quandary. If I said *no* then they would not want me as their priest. Who wants a priest not interested in growth? I also knew that you couldn't just snap your fingers and *voila*, new members appear. If I answered *yes* and the parish didn't grow, in a year I would be in trouble and probably be asked to leave. So I gave what I call a *pastoral answer*,

"Maybe," I said.

"Maybe?" Walter looked over in my direction.

"I can't promise that I'll grow the parish, but I'll try to serve you the best that I can, that's all I can do. We'll see what happens later." They stared at me for a moment. I wasn't used to people asking what I thought. In seminary no one asked for my opinion. I was used to keeping my head down and taking notes, not speaking my mind, especially regarding parish matters.

They were concerned about their immediate future. From what I heard at dinner, membership and morale were down. It was a small miracle that the parish was still functioning, especially after a long stream of short-term pastors: their previous pastor, Father Hank was ordained without college or seminary training. Father Randy was obese, had severe back problems, and often cancelled services. Father Jim was a nurse in Florida, who, like Father Hank drove up on weekends. Rumors were that he was also an alligator wrestler on the side. Father Joseph was here for six months and then left. According to parish records this parish went through six priests in nineteen years. If this date went well I'd be their seventh pastor, or victim, depending on how my odds turned out. It also occurred to me that I would be their first full-time, seminary-educated, residential pastor in over a decade.

Dessert and coffee were served and then they got down to practicalities, such as my living conditions. Walter started,

"From our previous correspondence we stated that we can only pay eighteen thousand a year plus pension," he said while looking over at the parish treasurer, "Isn't that right?" She nodded in agreement. I already knew that the pay was low and I was thinking about getting a part time job for a while. Of course Taisia would work too. I figured things would improve in a year or two. I had no choice, this had to work out.

He continued,

"A bunch of us were talking before you arrived and we thought you could stay in the back-building so you could save money."

The night before, Walter and Linda had shown me the back building, which was three small rooms, a concrete floor with area rugs, no running water, no kitchen, and no bathroom. One room was reserved for storage; the other was a makeshift bedroom with two metal cots pushed together to make a queen bed. Next to the bed was an upside-down milk crate with a lamp and alarm clock. The main room had a brown plastic foldout table, three folding chairs and a brown faux-wood computer desk. In the corner was an electric heater. Looking around I noticed the absence of a bathroom.

"No bathroom?" I asked.

"There's one in the Church, and they use the kitchen sink for washing. Walter wasn't smiling so I assumed he was serious. He bent down and showed me a five-gallon bucket next to the bed, "Father uses the slop pot at night."

This wasn't the *Dukes of Hazzard*, this was *The Beverly Hillbillies* meets *Little House on the Prarie*. This tour was going sour really fast.

"What about meals?" I asked.

"Margaret puts up a crockpot of beans on Friday night and they eat that all weekend."

Walter must have seen my initial reaction to the back building offer because he quickly followed up,

"No worries. We can spruce it up Father. We can install a commode, a stove, maybe put in a combo A/C unit. We can even add a few throw rugs if you want."

How can you spruce up a dump? A dump is a dump is a dump; Lowe's or no Lowe's, we weren't living on eighteen thousand a year *and* not in a shed.

"Well, I don't know, Walter . . ." I started.

He noticed my hesitation,

"If you don't like the back-building, I think we have enough money for a double wide. We can put it on the side yard and even put a deck on it."

First they want me to live in a glorified shed and now a double wide?

I didn't know what to think. I realize people lived in trailer parks, one of my aunts lived in one, but it was a nice one in south Florida. It had walking and biking trails and a small pool. But this wasn't a trailer park, it was a Church surrounded by homes on a busy street. I could just see my friends' reaction when I went back to New York and told them about my wonderful weekend: in-fighting congregation, low salary, and my choice of either a souped-up shed or a doublewide. I'd be the laughingstock of Crestwood.

I continued, "Thanks, for the offer, but I don't think my wife wants to live in a double wide." I wanted to add, *or a shed,* but I didn't. If I went home and told her we had two choices: either a trailer with a deck or a shed with no running water, she'd leave me.

And with that I took a bite of my dessert and a sip of coffee, hoping that we'd finish the meeting soon. I was exhausted.

I look back on my first date and laugh. It's surreal knowing what happened that weekend in December. Most guys would have taken one look and run the other way. However, I never thought of what the congregation must have thought of me; a sickly, nose running, twenty-seven-year-old pastor who could barely talk, who couldn't answer their simple questions. Why would they want to take a chance on me? I had no previous experience except for two short-term summer parish internships. I had no winning record at a previous parish. They were taking a big risk by saying yes to me.

I also realize how uncharitable I was. Rather than see the potential and the possibilities in the congregation I saw the drawbacks. I noticed what they didn't have rather than what they did have: a warm loving caring community who welcomed a young, very inexperienced pastor into their hearts and homes. Over time I learned that parish life is about community, not construction. Of course I would have liked a nicer physical plant, but the parish is about the people of God. I failed to see the dedication, hard work, love, and the many sacrifices that these families made in order to keep the parish afloat. I failed to see the goodwill of Walter and others who wanted to make the parish more welcoming for me and my family. Nativity wasn't Saint Patrick's, and not even close to Holy Resurrection, but they cared for their community just like they cared for their own children. It took me a long while to fully understand and appreciate what a parish community and pastoral ministry is all about. I realized that I would have a lot to learn, and the parish would teach me.

PART TWO

CHAPTER 8

Eye Opening

When I arrived one of the first things on my agenda was to set up an Adult Education program. If the congregation wanted to grow they needed to learn about their faith. I wanted to start with a book club. Book clubs were popular, everyone was hosting them: libraries, women's groups, neighborhoods, synagogues, and parishes. A book club would create community and foster fellowship. A book club would strengthen the Church. I chose Luke Timothy Johnson's *The Real Jesus*. Johnson was a New Testament professor at Candler School of Theology and wrote the book as a primer to the Jesus wars that were going on at the time. Scholars were debating the Jesus of history, *i.e.,* what we learn from the historical data, versus the Jesus of faith, what we learn about Jesus from the Bible. All the major news magazines highlighted the Jesus wars and Johnson was on television programs talking about his book and the Jesus debates. By choosing his book I was showing the parish that I had my finger on the pulse of the culture. I was creative. I was a pioneer. I assigned the book and everyone agreed to read it, or so I thought.

I envisioned this would be one of the many books we'd read together. I arranged a small parish lending library full of books, videos, and pamphlets about the Orthodox faith. We were going to be a learning community. Books would bring us together, unify us in our common longing for God and the divine. We would sip coffee and eat pastries and discuss the finer points of theology. This would become a mini version of seminary. I desired to share with them the beauty of our great Christian tradition. We would sit around on cold winter nights and discuss how we could become better Christians and deepen our faith. *Upwards and onwards,* I thought.

Our first session arrived and I was prepared. I'd taken copious notes and underlined sections of the book that we would discuss. I even made handouts to help with our discussions.

I started the class by leading them in the Lord's Prayer. After saying "*Amen,*" everyone sat down.

"It's really good to be here this evening," I said.

I noticed they had brought their books and one or two brought a notebook and pens. Someone else brought a Bible. I felt like a teacher on the first day of class. All that I needed was a briefcase and an apple and I'd be all set.

"So, before we get into the first chapter I'd like to ask: how did you like it?"

Some folks looked down at the table, others looked at each other. No one responded. I paused for a moment. Robert raised his hand.

"Yes," I said.

"I don't understand the title. Jesus is Jesus, right?"

"Well, kind of," I said.

A few people chuckled.

"Kind of?" Someone else asked.

"Yes, kind of. It depends on one's perspective." I was treading carefully. I wasn't sure whether they were well versed in the Jesus debates.

I continued, "Good point, Rob. According to Johnson, Jesus is not who we think he is."

I looked around and they were giving me the, *I have no idea what you're saying* face. I continued speaking slowly and clearly so they'd get the point.

"You know, the current debate about how Jesus was both human and divine, sift through the problems and particularities of how we understand Jesus."

Still blank faces.

Claire raised her hand.

"Yes, Claire," I said.

"Father, like Rob, I tried reading the first few pages but had to stop. I just couldn't follow."

"Couldn't follow what?" The book was written on a high school level.

"I found him a little dry."

Dry? Now I was getting irritated. Johnson was one of the best New Testament scholars in the field. He was quoted in the newspapers. He wrote for both the academy and the general public. Most importantly, *I* loved Johnson's work and they were going to love it too.

"Well, if you keep reading, Claire, you'll find that Johnson engages the reader, you know, he speaks for the common person."

Someone else raised their hand, "I don't get it when he says that we have little information about the Jesus of history. Jesus was a historical person, right?"

"Good question. What he means is that we have little information about Jesus outside of the Bible. We have a few Roman records concerning a person called Jesus Chrestus, or Jesus the Christ, as they say, but that's about it. We don't have enough information to write a biography like we do for Abraham Lincoln or Thomas Jefferson. For now we just have to go with what we have in the text."

I looked around the room and asked,

"Did everyone follow what I just said?"

Still blank looks. I was desperate for them to understand. By now I realized they agreed with Robert and Claire. I was going to do everything to convince them that this book was just what they needed whether they liked it or not.

"Okay, quick quiz. How many of you actually read the first two chapters for tonight?"

No hands went up.

"What about at least chapter one?" I continued.

Two people raised their hand.

"Curious—did *anyone* read whole the book?"

John's hand went up, "I can probably speak for everyone here," he said while looking at the others, "when I say that most of us are busy, work, errands, dinner, kids. We just don't have a lot of time, especially to read a book, any book, let alone this one."

A few heads nodded in agreement.

Didn't they realize that most of my seminary classmates were married and had children? *They* found time to take care of their families *and* read books. Why couldn't my parishioners do the same? What was their excuse?

Someone else raised their hand.

"Yes?" I said.

"You know, it might not be a bad idea. Why don't you just tell us what the book says, you know, give us the highlights?"

If they wanted highlights they should read the *The Bible for Dummies*.

I thought we were going to read books and grow and learn about Jesus, the gospels, and God. Forget about the book club, I needed to focus on Bible 101. I don't know why I was so shocked. I never read the Bible or books about Jesus until I entered seminary. Mom or Dad never read the Bible either. It wasn't until later that I fell in love with Scripture. I wanted others to fall in love with it too. Maybe I was going about this in the wrong way? Maybe I needed to start with the basics rather than go full force with a book club? I made a mental note for later.

I had no idea about the challenges of family life. Taisia and I didn't have children yet. We didn't have to help with homework, wait in line for carpool or after school activities. We didn't have to pack lunches or eat and run in order to get our children to a sports event. We had it easy compared with other families in the congregation. I had a lot to learn and unfortunately it wouldn't be easy. For many people going to a parish book club was way down on their list. I tried to envision my own mother going to a parish book club after working eight to ten long hours on her feet in the hospital, coming home to quickly change and grab a sandwich and then fight traffic for twenty miles in order to go talk about a book that she barely had time to read. No. I was going about this the wrong way.

That night also taught me another important lesson. I realized that this was *my* plan and *my* agenda and *my* ideas. I never asked *them* what they wanted to learn or what *they* were interested in or what *they* thought about the Bible. While some people enjoyed reading the Bible and were faithful in their prayer life, I quickly learned that many others weren't as faithful or committed. Yet they kept showing up Sunday after Sunday. They found solace and comfort in Church, but it wasn't for the book club, that's for sure. I wanted them to understand why a strong and vibrant faith was important for their life.

I also failed to realize that they had been living and praying together long before I arrived. I thought that I was their teacher, but little did I know that *they* were going to teach me more than *I* was going to teach them. They already had a common life and shared a common history. I was an outsider. I was a priest but not yet a pastor.

We eventually ditched the book club. They said they'd like to have a Faith and Film Series instead, where we'd watch a modern movie with a spiritual theme and we would have a casual conversation over light refreshments. They asked me if I was interested in leading the discussions. I agreed. We were happy.

CHAPTER 9

I Signed Up for This?

Some seminarians might have been well trained but not this one. Even though I knew the ins and outs of academic theology, I didn't have experience running a meeting, let alone creating an agenda, reading a financial statement, leading small groups, or implementing the annual stewardship and pledge drives. Funny thing was that at the time I didn't realize how little I knew.

Walter was the parish council warden, sometimes referred to as the parish council president. I was too embarrassed to tell the council that I had never led a meeting so I simply asked Walter if he could create the agenda. My excuse was that I was too distracted and tired from unpacking and settling in to our new apartment, which was in fact, true. He agreed. When I arrived everyone gathered in the hall and someone made coffee and put out a tray of cookies and pastries.

Walter walked around the table distributing copies of the agenda. I looked over at Walter and asked him where I should sit,

"Since you're the priest you should sit at the head of the table." He pointed to the side with only one chair.

I stood there for a moment,

"I kinda just wanted to sit with everyone else," I said.

"No, no, no, Father. You're in charge now," he said with a grin. Everyone was looking in my direction. In seminary I was just one of the crowd, all this attention made me feel uncomfortable. I never knew what it felt like to be in charge because I had never been in charge of anything before.

Administrators and professors are in charge of things, not students. I kept forgetting that even though I was very young, the fact that I had the title Father and wore a clergy collar and cassock meant that now I was in charge of this congregation. It would take years for me to realize this too.

Even though I was their spiritual leader I considered myself a part of the parish community. I wasn't above them or apart from them, but one of them. I reluctantly walked over to my chair and looking down, noticed a wooden gavel resting on the table. I picked it up and before I could say anything Walter started.

"Oh, Father Hank left it for you."

"For what?" I asked.

"Order in the court, order in the court!" A council member piped up.

"Yeah, like Judge Judy," someone else said.

This was going to be a long evening. I felt like someone had plopped me in a boat, given me a fishing pole, and said: *Here, fish.*

I pushed the gavel aside. I knew this was part of their normal protocol, but I couldn't follow it. It's one thing if you're leading a meeting of six hundred, quite another for a meeting of six.

I looked at my watch: seven o'clock. I began, "Okay, I think we should start, lets stand up and open the meeting with prayer."

Everyone bowed their heads. I led them in a short prayer asking God for guidance and direction. I paused, seeing that this was a historic moment, my first meeting with my first parish council. At the end of the prayer we all sat down.

I looked at the agenda. "First thing we need to do is accept the minutes from the June meeting, isn't that right?" I said looking over at Walter for confirmation. I didn't know what else to say so I just sat there saying nothing.

Walter chimed in. "Father, we need to call a vote."

"Vote for what?" I asked.

"To accept the June minutes."

"Oh."

Silence. Walter jumped in, "Father, you need to call the vote before we move on."

"Not sure how to do that."

"You don't?"

"No."

"Okay, I'll do it then. All in favor of accepting the June minutes say aye," Walter said with a sigh.

"Aye," everyone said.

I wasn't used to all the, *Father this* and *Father that*. Even after my ordination my friends called me Bill. Mom and Dad called me Billy, but here people called me *Father*, "Good morning *Father*," or "How are you doing today *Father*," or "See you next week *Father*." I was too young to be called Father. A Father was someone older, wiser, and had grey hair, crow's feet and a slight paunch. A Father was someone with life experience. A Father had warts and wrinkles. A Father had gravitas and wisdom. In my mind I wasn't a Father.

As the treasurer started talking I looked down at the spreadsheet. On the left were words like checking and savings, building fund, pledges, income statement, profit and loss, cash on hand, CD, Altar fund, choir fund, brotherhood and sisterhood fund. On the right were lists of numbers, some had brackets around them, others had asterisks with footnotes on the bottom of the page. Some lines had plus signs next to them and others had minus signs. I quickly figured that the building fund was allocated for the building and that the monies in the checking and savings were for spending, but the rest? I didn't have a clue. As the treasurer guided us through the spreadsheet I kept saying, "Uh, huh" and "Umm" and nodded even though I had no idea what was going on. I became a good actor.

Marianne raised her hand. She was in her mid-fifties with blondish grey hair cut in a bob.

"I have something that I wanna bring up."

I looked down at the agenda and noticed that her name was not under new business. I looked over at Walter for what I should do. He nodded showing that it was okay for her to continue.

"It's about coffee hour," she said.

"Okay, go on," I said.

"Some weeks we have lots of food, but other weeks, well, there's not much."

She continued, "Rather than have a potluck every Sunday, I was thinking that we could get a bunch of bagels and butter, keep it simple. That's what they did up north, coffee and bagels, no fuss, no muss."

"Not my parish, we only had bread and butter, no bagels, just bread and butter," someone said.

Someone else butted in, "But who's going to get the bagels? We need someone to do that."

"We can take a survey," Walter suggested.

"A survey?" I piped up.

"We need to know who likes raisin or whole grain," someone said jokingly.

I offered a half-hearted grin. I sat there looking at Marianne talk about bagels. She didn't seem to be joking either. I couldn't believe what I was hearing. I assumed we'd be talking about evangelism, outreach, missions, and ministries, not about bagels or bread and butter.

Marianne continued, "We could just have a whole bunch of bagels in the freezer. That way someone can buy them once every two months."

"I don't like frozen bagels," someone said. "Taste like cardboard."

"Yeah, me too. I like them fresh, with peanut butter and jelly!"

Walter turned and looked over in my direction, "What do you think, Father?"

"I guess everyone has a different experience with this type of thing and from what I gather there are people here who have been bringing casseroles and cakes and cookies, so I can't imagine telling them not to bring those things. It's a gift, no? A donation of their time and energy?"

"Yeah, but I can't cook like Mary does. I can't bring homemade cheesecakes like she makes," Marianne said, looking directly at me. "I work all week, I can't go out and spend half my Saturday shopping and cooking for Church, I'm tired," she said. "Coming on Sunday is enough for me, I can't do much else."

"But you don't have to bring anything if you don't want to," I said. "If people want to bring food, let them bring food."

"The problem is it's feast or famine. Some weeks there's tons of food and others, well, just cookies and coffee. We need consistency. We need order around here."

"Bagels are fine by me," someone chimed in. "Yeah, me too. I'm tired of bringing food, too much work."

There was a moment of silence. I realized it was futile to banter about bagels all night. It also sounded like some people were of two minds. I didn't know how to solve this problem.

"Well, I think we need to survey the parish after Sunday services. See what the congregation thinks. What do you think, Father?" Walter asked.

I didn't know what to say, but somehow I blurted out, "I guess we could do a survey if you all want." I didn't think a survey would solve the problem but I went along with it anyway. Food is food, who cares if folks bring mac-n-cheese or a tuna noodle casserole?

I wasn't sure what had just transpired. We ended the meeting with a big question looming: were we going to have bagels and butter or were people going to continue bringing regular food?

I led a short closing prayer. People hugged and shook hands. Someone unplugged the coffee pot. Someone else emptied the trash can. I helped move the tables and chairs back to where they belonged. I locked the Church and walked over to my car. The sweet smell of honeysuckle and orange blossoms was strong in the late summer evening. I got into my car, turned on the air conditioner and pulled out of the driveway. While heading home I kept replaying the bagel conversation over in my head. These were parish leaders and we had just had a thirty-minute debate about bagels and butter. I'd studied hard and written term papers. I had gotten good grades. Yet I couldn't read a spreadsheet or a financial report. I worked great alone, but I had no idea how to work with real people and real problems. My theological training was theoretical, but not very practical. I didn't understand why Marianne had such a passion for bagels and butter? Why couldn't she let things go the way they were going? If she didn't want to she didn't have to stay for coffee hour. If she did stay for coffee hour she could bring a cake. Why the long debate and discussion?

I was frustrated. I wished I had more leadership skills. What I really wanted to say to Marianne was, *are you serious*? But of course I didn't. The fact was that she was serious and that's what was so shocking to me. I felt overwhelmed and underequipped. I wanted to show that I could lead, but I didn't know what to do. They kept asking my opinion, but I didn't have one. I was too new, too fresh out of seminary to have any deep thoughts of my own. We never discussed parish council meetings at seminary. If I shared this with my congregation they wouldn't believe me. I learned to play my cards close, trying to put on a poker face while I had no idea what I was doing.

I soon realized that many conversations would be similar to the one I had that summer evening. I would sit and listen to debates and heated discussions about who was going to cook the hotdogs and hamburgers at the annual picnic or whether or not we should have purple or blue table cloths for the parish dinner. I noticed that the smallest agenda items usually required the longest and most detailed discussions. Even after all these years of ministry I've never gotten used to it, I often sit there wondering to myself, "Did I sign up for this?"

CHAPTER 10

Can Someone Pass Me a Hammer?

Before arriving at the parish, I couldn't tell the difference between PVC and HVAC or a two-by-four or a four-by-four. It was all the same to me. My father wasn't Tim the Tool Man. He was Don the Dummy. If we had a leaky faucet he'd call a plumber. If we had an electrical problem he called an electrician. When the house needed painting he called a painter. All Dad did was change a light bulb or two and stain our front and back porch every other year. One summer the both of us painted the garage. He called it bonding. I called it purgatory.

God has a sense of humor. One of my first duties was helping with construction. According to the New Testament we know that Joseph, Jesus' earthly father, was a carpenter and it's most likely that Jesus followed in Joseph's footsteps. Jesus may have been in construction but I wasn't Jesus. My soft supple hands were familiar with books and Bibles, but not with saws and shovels. I knew a little about painting and power washing from college summer jobs, but that was the extent of my experience. I wasn't ready for hard labor; and I mean *hard*: mixing concrete, laying tile, painting, and landscaping. I thought I was supposed to be a preacher and teacher, not a day laborer. It was baptism by fire.

On the first Saturday of every month a group of men gathered at Church to do odd jobs: changing light bulbs, doing yard work, installing mulch, and various other tasks. Sometimes they power washed the building and other times they trimmed trees. The men said that they did it for fellowship. I think they wanted to escape their wives.

The day started around eight o'clock with coffee and donuts and ended around one or two with lunch. Since I was their new pastor I thought it would be good to join them. I didn't want to go but I thought it was important to show my support and leadership.

Sam was our resident contractor and I knew enough to let him take the lead. I didn't know anything about construction and I knew that someone else needed to be in charge. Thankfully he agreed.

One of the first projects on our list was to move water away from the building. When it rained, water pooled around the foundation, damaging the siding. Sam suggested that we install a French drain. I knew about French fries, French toast, and French bread, but not French drains. He wanted to connect the downspout that started at the end of the gutters and came down the length of the building to a long hard plastic pipe that would take the water from the roof all the way across the parking lot and into the grassy area at the edge of our property. We would bury the pipe under ground. Rather than pay a professional we would do the work ourselves. The parish functioned with a modest budget so we had to cut corners. Labor was the first place to cut. No problem I thought, I've dug holes before. This would be easy.

I showed up dressed in shorts, sneakers, and a t-shirt. I also brought a pair of work gloves. I was proud. I was their new priest. I was there to show solidarity and leadership. We were building community.

I didn't want to make the wrong impression by showing up late so I made sure I was early. I unlocked the Church, turned on the lights and got some coffee going. Sam arrived a few minutes after me, then a few others straggled in later.

I surveyed the room and noticed a lot of men were missing; only six showed up, where were the others? For three weeks Sam had made announcements and I'd also put the information in the bulletin. I was angry that only six people came. I had heard about the eighty-twenty rule in parish life; twenty percent give most of the money and do most of the work. I thought that pertained to *other* parishes, not *mine*. We were all in this together through thick and thin. I was wrong.

We finally got down to business. Sam told me I would be working with Walter. By now I knew Walter pretty well. He and Linda helped us move into our apartment and we had already had dinner at their house a few times. Linda helped arrange our apartment kitchen. She purchased cabinet liners for our cabinets. Walter and I took long walks on the local greenway and went out to lunch. Walter helped me move furniture into our new house and spent a lot of time with me during my first weeks and months at the parish. Since Walter was almost thirty years older than I was, I deferred to him often, seeking his guidance and advice. I often consulted with him and sought his support with parish problems. I trusted him.

Our first job was to rake a two-foot-wide path across the parking lot so that we could dig the trench with the Ditch Witch. A Ditch Witch looks about five times as large as a regular push lawn mower but with larger wheels. However, unlike a lawn mower the Ditch Witch has a diamond edged saw to cut through concrete and rock.

Sam gave us instructions,

"You pull the cord here like a lawn mower." He bent down with one hand, put his foot on top of the machine and pulled on the cord. Small puffs of grey smoke rose from the motor. It was noisy. I hadn't brought earplugs. He continued, "Then you press the button which lowers the cutter and then one person holds the bar here and then another person holds the side here."

"Okay?"

Walter and I nodded. I had no idea what to do but I went along with him. I trusted both of them more than I trusted myself.

Sam continued, "When you're done you turn it off and then after lunch we'll install the pipe." Sam turned down the throttle a bit.

"Okay boss man," Walter laughed. I put on my work gloves.

Sam got some of the other guys started on other odd jobs, a few were power washing the Church building, and some were painting. He walked across the parking lot and got into his truck and headed for Lowe's to buy more materials. Walter and I were on our own. He started the machine and held onto the bar. I braced the Ditch With on the side like Sam showed us.

The blade kicked up dirt and dust making both of us cough. The machine was so loud we couldn't talk, so I just stood next to Walter bracing the machine while he maneuvered the levers.

It was around ten o'clock and the sun was already high over the horizon. I wasn't ready for the Carolina heat. Summers in New York were hot but not hot *and* humid. Sweat pooled at the back of my neck and dripped down my t-shirt. I hadn't brought a hat and made a mental note to bring one next time. I also forgot to wear sunscreen. I didn't realize how unprepared I was; no earplugs, no hat, no sunscreen, and no jeans. I would never last a day on a real job site. I was only a few hours into my first one and I was hot, tired, sweaty, and my muscles ached. After two hours I was ready to quit. Did Sam work these guys hard like this every month? I realized that I'd better get used to this soon otherwise, I'd be in trouble.

A truck pulled into the driveway kicking up dirt and stone. It was Sam. He looked over in our direction, pulled down his window and said something inaudible.

Getting out of his truck, he waved his arms, yelling something, but we still couldn't hear.

"Stop, stop," I heard as he walked closer.

"What?" I shouted back.

"Look," Sam said as he pointed at the ground.

Walter and I looked down.

The Ditch Witch had dug a three-foot deep hole but it wasn't a trench. Sam pointed at the gearshift, it was in park. We never shifted it into drive. No wonder the machine was so hard to move. Walter and I laughed while I wiped more sweat off my neck. Sam managed to get a laugh out too, saying that you get what you pay for.

In late November we started another building project. Everyone agreed that the parish needed some repair work so we made a master list of several jobs that needed to be done. After a few meetings we agreed on the tasks. We would install new tile in the Education Building which was originally where Father Hank stayed. We would hire professionals to knock down the wall and do the electrical and plumbing work but we'd do the rest. We also wanted to install a sidewalk around the Church. All of this sounded wonderful, but we were parishioners, not contractors. What was I getting myself into? I was doing more construction work than I was hearing confessions. My fingers had callouses.

Sam stood in the front of the Education building surveying the wooden form that he had already put up for the new front stoop,

"This is going to be great, a nice porch for the kids," I said.

"Yep," he replied, still looking at a piece of paper." He was marking down some numbers on a small lined pad.

"Whaddya doing?" I said.

"Oh, just seeing how much cement we'll need. I bought some extra just in case." He continued writing down numbers.

I looked around and saw some garden shovels, a long green hose, and about twenty bags of concrete mix off to the side,

"So where's the mixer?" I asked.

"No mixer. We're doing it by hand."

"By hand?"

"It's easier. Mixer is too hard to use and this is a small stoop."

"You mean we're going to mix all that?" I pointed over to the pile of bags,

"Yep, all twenty. Fifty pounds each."

"Oh my gosh. . ." I put my hand over my heart feigning a heart attack. He interrupted before I could finish,

"Don't worry Father. With you, Walter, Bob, and Larry, we'll be done in no time."

Sam and his crew built a seven-foot by five-foot form that was about sixteen inches deep. He added gravel at the bottom to provide support. All of us were standing around with shovels, not knowing what would come next. Sam had more faith in us than we had in ourselves.

"Okay, I'm going to dump these bags into the form and then I'll start adding water." Sam said.

We glanced over at the hose then back over at Sam.

"When the water hits you have to start mixing. We have to work fast otherwise the cement won't cure right. Okay?"

"Okay, boss man," some of the guys said.

"So why are *you* holding the hose and not mixing?" Someone asked.

"I'm in charge," Sam said with a grin.

He slowly turned on the water and began spraying the dry cement mixture. As soon as the water hit the concrete it turned into a grey soupy muddy mess. We mixed it with our shovels. Sam kept adding water. The more we mixed the harder the mixture became. We mixed and we mixed and we mixed. We were like three witches stirring our brew. My shoulders ached. My back ached. My legs ached. My hands were getting chapped from the cold weather. I had forgotten my work gloves. "Harder guys, you gotta mix harder, we don't have much time. Cement settles quickly." We mixed for about thirty minutes. There was no more dry powder. It was all evenly grey and evenly soupy. "Perfect," Sam said. He walked over to his truck and brought back a hand-held, flat cement trowel about two feet long by nine or ten inches wide.

"Now, you guys can watch an artist at work," he said while getting down on both knees.

"Yeah, yeah, yeah," we replied in unison nudging each other with our arms.

"Not artist, but *artiste*," Bob said drawing out the final syllable like it was French.

Sam went back and forth like he was icing a cake. When he was done he made two three bar Orthodox crosses in the cement on either side of the stoop.

After the Education Building project was finished, we added an extension to the main Church building and installed new carpet. Over the course of two weeks Walter and I painted the entire sanctuary. We installed new chandeliers and ceiling tiles, and added space to our coffee hour area. We also paved our parking lot and installed a new sign in front of the Church. We built a playground for the children and added flowerbeds around the Church and Education building. I can't count how much money we saved and how many work hours were involved. Looking back it still boggles my mind how we did it all.

Over the years I learned how to install mulch, hang doors, plant trees and shrubs, paint parking lot lines by hand, and use a power washer and circular saw. I pulled weeds and planted bulbs. Now I have more than enough experience for a contractor's license.

When I drive into the parking lot on Sunday morning I often think of the love and tenderness that was put into this parish. Yes, it would have been easier to pay someone else to do it, but it would have been more expensive. While we worked together we also shared our stories, our pains, our joys, and our hopes and fears. We offended, but we also forgave. We weren't just caring for our property, we were caring for our community. I know that we drove Sam crazy. He was used to working with professionals. Yet he took all of this in stride showing us that while a project may seem overwhelming, it was doable. He believed in us. Now we believe in ourselves.

We no longer have our monthly workdays, we've changed to having them a few times a year. Most of our parish members are under forty and are busy with family and work. I no longer have to worry about who will or won't show up, we always have a good turnout with twenty or thirty people. I arrive early, put on a pot of coffee and someone else brings donuts. I learned to accept life as it comes, not as I wish it would be. I learned that my job isn't to change people, but to encourage and inspire them, that's all I can do. For some people the parish is our spiritual home and we work hard to take care of it like we would our own home. Other people just show up on Sunday morning, say their prayers, have a bite to eat and leave. For me, community is bonding, a sharing that requires solidarity in the good, the bad, and the ugly. It means showing up for Sunday services and for a Wednesday evening funeral. It means showing up for a Church picnic and a Saturday workday. It also means going to Lowe's to pick up a few items needed at Church, and thankfully, now I know the difference between PVC and HVAC.

Sunday Morning Marathon

When I was young our Sundays were like most people's: go to Church, pray, and go home. However, I quickly learned that Sundays are *very different* for pastors.

On Sunday morning the alarm goes off at six-thirty. I hit the snooze button at least once, burrowing back under the covers for a few more minutes. I look over at my wife, tucked warmly under our white down comforter. I'm jealous. She, like everyone else, gets to sleep a few more winks, but I have to get up and go to work. Sundays are for sleeping in, at least that's what my un-churched friends tell me. After all, for them it's their weekend. For me, it's my big workday. I often wonder what it feels like sleeping late, having breakfast, lounging around in pajamas, reading the paper, or taking a walk in the park.

After shaving and brushing my teeth I take a shower. On weekdays my shower thoughts revolve around the events for the coming day: grocery shopping, menus for the week, and bills that need to be paid. On Sundays my shower thoughts are on the sermon.

People expect a well-crafted and inspiring sermon, preferably under ten minutes long. Beginnings and endings of sermons are important. "Today in the gospel reading from John. . ." No that sounds too boring, maybe I'll begin with a funny story, "Did you hear the one about the priest and the rabbi who walk into the bar?" Nah. How about, "Jesus calls us to be faithful disciples. . ." Yes, that's a good opener.

By seven o'clock I walk into our closet. Most men worry about matching their ties and shirts. Not me. Instead of a tie I wear a collar, a thin white piece of plastic that looks like a tongue depressor. I'm not sure who came up with the collar. Anglican priests used to wear fancy white-laced scarves under their preaching robes, signifying that they were members of the clergy. Over time the scarf morphed into a white plastic tab. So now clergy wear white tongue depressors rather than scarfs. I'd rather wear a scarf.

Each clergy shirt comes with two collars. I own ten, which means I have at least twenty tongue depressors floating around the house and car. Every once in a while I find one under my car seat or on the closet floor. After I die my children and grandchildren will find collars in the most unexpected places. At least they'll remember me. I hope.

Clergy shirts traditionally come in three colors: black, grey, or white. Recently they added blue denim for pastors who desire that Roy Rogers look. Not me. I don't see myself going to Church looking like I just got off the rodeo. I'll stick with black for the time being.

My choices for Sunday mornings are limited: either a black clergy shirt with charcoal colored pants or a grey clergy shirt with black pants. At Easter I usually wear grey pants and a white shirt. There's one golden rule that I always keep: never, never, never, do I wear either *all* black or *all* white, I don't want to look like Marcel Marceau or even worse, Captain Steubing from the *Love Boat*. I know my clothing choices are limited, but what can I do?

By seven-thirty I begin the twenty-minute car drive down to Church. During weekdays traffic is unbearable, but there are few vehicles on the road this early on Sunday morning. I love driving across Lake Norman, especially during the fall all and winter months, when the early morning fog slowly lifts and the sun begins to rise and sometimes I'll see a flock of Canada geese flying high above as a reminder that the colder months are coming. Driving allows me some quiet time to collect my thoughts and to review the sermon a few more times before the service begins later that morning.

I don't preach from notes, so when I stand before the congregation, I need to know the sermon very well. I repeat my thoughts in my head numerous times until the words flow like water from a waterfall, naturally and effortlessly. Parishioners deserve the best and I try to give them my best. Do I succeed? Sometimes yes, and sometimes no. I'll let God be the judge of that.

Around eight o'clock I arrive at the parking lot. Our parish doesn't have a staff so I have to do a lot of work. The work isn't hard but it's time consuming, a lot of little things that need to get done before the people arrive. After unlocking the door I turn off the alarm and turn on the lights. I write the weekly announcements on the wipe board, mostly newsy stuff or prayer requests. I then walk into the kitchen, open the freezer and take out the bread that I will use for Communion. The bread is the size of a large Frisbee and is about six inches thick. Once a month I'll bake the bread that we use in worship: seven pounds of flour, seven cups of warm water, a teaspoon of yeast, mix well, let rise for an hour, punch down, put in the oven for forty-five minutes, and voilá, two large loaves of bread.

While the bread thaws I boil water in a hot pot. Before communion time I'll mix the warm water and the wine together, which symbolizes that Jesus was both divine and human. After the water boils I make sure that we have enough candles in the candle box and that the prayer books are neatly arranged. Candles are a symbol of prayer and people light candles for friends or family members who are sick, suffering, or traveling. After doing all of this I wipe away any eye gunk or lint from my clothes. Now I'm ready to put on my vestments, or as one little girl once told me, my costume. She's right, sometimes it feels like a costume.

People treat you differently when you wear clergy clothes. Once a pizza guy offered me a free soda and then another time, while driving on the Pennsylvania Turnpike, I got out of a speeding ticket. I thanked God *all* the way home. Yet it bothers me that people treat me differently because I wear clergy clothes and have a fancy title. If I'm at a social function and people find out that I'm a minister they often don't know what to say. They either quickly change the conversation or suddenly feel the need to ask me about death and dying. When someone asks me what I do for a living I am tempted to say, "life insurance," and then walk away. Why can't people talk to me as just another person and accept me for who I am rather than seeing only my role as a pastor? I still can't understand that.

My vestments hang in a closet near the Altar. They are lined with matching-colored satin and trimmed with gold brocades. A set of well-made vestments costs anywhere between one thousand and fifteen hundred dollars and can last twenty years if they are regularly dry-cleaned. I still have my original set that was given to me at my ordination. They look just as good now as when I first wore them. Thankfully they still fit too.

As I put on each article of clothing I recite certain verses from scripture. I first put on a long, ankle-length white robe and say the following:

> *My soul shall rejoice in the Lord for He has clothed me with the garment of salvation; He has covered me with the robe of gladness; as a bridegroom He has set a crown on me; and as a bride adorns herself with jewels, so He has adorned me. (Isaiah 61:10)*

The white robe symbolizes baptism. When babies are baptized they are given a white robe. White is also a symbol of purity. More often than not I don't feel pure. Actually, I never feel pure, but the white robe reminds me to keep working harder towards that goal.

After the robe I put on a stole, a longish vestment that goes around my neck and hangs down the front of my chest and almost to the top of my shoes:

> *Blessed is God, who pours down His grace upon His priests, as myrrh upon the head, that runs down the beard, the beard of Aaron, that runs down the border of his robe.(Psalm 133:1–2)*

Then I put on a five-inch-wide fabric belt that looks like something Superman would wear. The belt ties behind my back with two thin pieces of material:

> *Blessed is God who girds me with strength and makes my way blameless. He made my feet like hinds feet, and sets me secure on the heights. (Psalm 18:33–34)*

Strength. Yes. I need strength, lots of strength. Most of the time I feel weak and helpless. I often lack direction. Parishioners look to me for pearls of wisdom. They think I'm smart and have lots of experience, but the truth is that I often feel like I'm making it up as I go. I have more questions than answers and I have plenty of doubts about God, the Church, and ministry. Yet I still forge ahead.

Then I put on two cuffs on my forearm, first my right hand and then my left:

> *Thy right hand, O Lord, has been glorified in power. Thy right hand, O Lord, has shattered the enemies. In the greatness of Thy majesty Thou hast overthrown thy adversaries. (Right hand) (Exodus 15:6–7)*

> *Thy hands have made and fashioned me. Give me understanding that I may learn Thy commandments. (Left hand) (Psalm 119:73)*

Then I put on my pectoral cross. I have three of them, a wooden one, a silver one, and a gold one. Priests have too much jewelry if you ask me. The cross goes over my head and hangs halfway down my chest:

> *The Lord said if anyone shall be my disciple He should take up his cross and follow me. (Matthew 16:24)*

Finally I put on a long outer garment called a chasuble, it looks like a cape and part of it comes to my mid-chest:

> *Thy priests, O Lord, shall clothe themselves with righteousness, and Thy saints shall rejoice with joy always, now and ever and unto ages of ages. Amen.*

At the conclusion of the vesting there is a ceremonial hand washing. I wash my hands in the sink adjacent to the Altar and recite the following:

> *I wash my hands in innocence, and go about Thy altar, O Lord, singing aloud a song of praise, and telling of all Thy miracles. O Lord I love the beauty of Thy house, and the place where Thy glory dwells. Do not sweep my soul away with sinners, nor my life with bloodthirsty men, in whose hands are evil devices, and whose right hands are full of bribes. But as for me, I walk in my integrity, deliver me, and have mercy on me. My foot stands on level ground; in the churches I will bless the Lord. (Psalm 26:6–12)*

I'm done. The vesting takes about five minutes but I don't rush, it gives me time to mentally prepare for the service and to reflect on the next ninety minutes. Vesting is like athletes putting on their uniforms before the game. I'd much rather wear a simple cassock and stole for services. All this gold and brocade is a bit much. Deep down I'm a low-Church kind of guy in a very high-Church world. Saint Paul never had to wear all this Byzantine bling, so why should I? But I'm not Saint Paul and times are different. Yet I submit myself to our tradition and customs and put on my robes.

After vesting I then walk into the Altar area to a small table which is called the table of oblation that is located on the side of the Atlar table. This is where I prepare the bread and wine that will be used during the service. On the table there are two crystal cruets, one containing wine and the other containing water. There is a golden chalice, which holds about three cups of wine. To the left of the chalice is a large golden plate called a *diskos*, which sits on a pedestal. The bread for Communion will be placed in the center of the *diskos* and then later it will be cut up for the congregation.

First I cut out a large five-inch square piece of bread from the center of the larger loaf and put it in the center of the *diskos*. I use a small paring knife, like the ones used for cutting vegetables, and then take out small, quarter-inch square pieces of bread in memory of important people in the life of the Church: the Virgin Mary, various saints (holy men and women), as well as pieces of bread in remembrance of the sick and suffering and those who have died. This symbolism reminds us that on Sunday morning the entire community gathers around the Altar, offering their common prayer and praise to God: the living, the departed, the saints, and the sinners alike.

It's now nine o'clock. Many of my neighbors are just waking up. Some are planning a leisurely Sunday brunch, others a jog, and some are headed to the lake for a boat ride. Over the years I have turned down countless invitations to Sunday parties, social gatherings, and outings. It's hard saying no all the time especially when everyone else is saying yes. Childhood memories flood back, Mom forbidding me to attend Saturday night sleepovers or soccer games because I couldn't miss Sunday services. While being a pastor has many rich blessings and joys, there's also the other side that I still find challenging. Most people work during the weekdays and are off weekends. They can choose to take a weekend getaway to the mountains or the beach, but I can't. They can choose to stay home or go to the lake. Not me. You may think this is trite but it's not trite when your boss is God and he requires you to work weekends and some evenings. It's not trite when you keep saying no to things, things that deep down you really would love to do. It's not trite when over time anger and resentment build up, when you say no to the dinner party you'd love to attend because you have a parish council meeting, or no to the last minute three-day beach trip. It's not trite when your family has spring break and would love to get away but you can't go because you have to lead services that week. It's not trite when you have a lovely birthday dinner planned for your spouse but you're five hundred miles away at a clergy conference that you have to attend.

The lector begins reading the Hours, a series of Psalms that are chanted before the Liturgy begins. As the reader begins I hear the back door opening and closing. People are now coming into Church. Orthodox worship can be chaotic. People coming in late, lighting candles, kissing icons, there is movement everywhere. I hear voices in the hall, people in the kitchen getting ready for our post Liturgy luncheon. Sometimes I hear a child crying or playing with toys. Some folks come in with shirt and tie and dresses and skirts, others come to Church in less formal attire. To a visitor this all may seem like organized chaos. Someone once told me that the parish feels like their living room, it's casual and comfortable. I think sometimes it's a bit too comfortable, but this is how it is.

I begin to cense the Church. In the ancient world incense was offered as a form of prayer and praise to the gods. Many religious traditions use incense in one way or another. The incense that we use is made up of various resins that are cooked together and then rolled into sweet smelling pellets that look like cat food rolled in baby powder. Little puffs of smoke rise from the censer as I swing it back and forth, the congregation now smells like a flower garden. As I cense around the sanctuary I notice all of the parishioners, old, young, men, women, adults, and children. Every so often we'll have a visitor or two. When I'm done censing I put the censer away and take a few moments and collect my thoughts.

It's nine thirty and it's show time. I begin the opening prayer: "Blessed is the Kingdom of the Father, and of the Son, and of the Holy Spirit." There's no stopping. No coffee break and no bathroom break. For a solid ninety minutes I'm in the spotlight, it's like playing basketball with no time-outs. I can't leave the Altar, except of course if I get deathly sick; *the show must go on,* as they say. Some people describe Orthodox worship like a symphony, each member of the congregation has their unique part. My role is to lead the congregation in prayer. Each prayer concludes with a "Lord have mercy" from the choir. Our choir is *a capella,* so there are no musical instruments, piano, or organ accompaniment. For ninety minutes I pray, the choir responds. We pray for the sick, for travelers, for the president and government officials, for good weather, for the armed forces, you name it, we pray for it. Worship is not just what I'm doing up in the Altar, but what goes on in the community. All of our prayers are in the plural: *we* pray, *we* bless, *we* give thanks. Worship is a communal act, one which involves heads and hearts alike.

The reader then reads from one of Paul's letters, which is followed by a Gospel reading. After the Gospel, I'll deliver the sermon. When I preach the choir has a ten-minute break, they sit and listen and rest their voices. I look out over the congregation, most of whom are looking at me and presumably are paying attention, some people come late and hang around in the back of the Church, and others look at their watches or out the window. I wonder what they're thinking. Do they really want to be here? Are they bored? Do they understand what's going on? Do they care? It's hard to tell what they're thinking. I guess I'll never know. Kids sit on the floor or run out for a potty break.

Some days I feel like I hit a home run, other times I feel like I just got to first base. There are days when I've felt like I gave a lousy sermon and someone comes up to me at the end of the service and says, "Father, thank you for your words today. It hit me in the heart." I'm grateful that my words helped them in some way. Other times I feel like I gave a stellar sermon and no one tells me anything. Go figure. In the end it's all up to God, I just keep repeating the same words that Jesus said, just in a slightly different way to keep it more interesting so that they come back the following week. Deep down I wish that they had to prepare a sermon once in a while so that they could see how hard it is. It may look easy, but trust me, it's hard, hard work.

Eleven o'clock, the service ends. After all the prayers and petitions, amens and alleluias, a sermon and announcements, we have coffee hour and we pig out; and I mean it, we eat well. Orthodox Christians fast from midnight until communion, so by eleven o'clock we're hungry. No juice and cookies, we have a full luncheon: macaroni-and-cheese, franks and beans, sausage and peppers, perhaps a soup or two, breads and bagels, chips and salsa, assorted desserts and fruit trays, and plates of crackers and dips. Our meals reflect the cultural diversity of our congregation: sometimes its chicken curry and naan bread, other days it may be homemade dumplings and borscht. Coffee social is a time for people to catch up and share their pains, problems, and joys. We talk about the weather, about our children, and about the coming events in our life. What begins in the sanctuary at nine concludes in the kitchen at eleven.

People don't realize it, and theologians don't often write about it, but coffee hour is a natural extension of the Liturgy and is just as sacramental as what takes place in the sanctuary. John Chrysostom calls it the *liturgy after the liturgy*; the sharing of the same food, the sharing of stories, of ones pains, problems, and joys, becomes the glue that binds a community together. It's wonderful to see old and young, newcomers and old timers alike break bread together after the services. Yes it's chaotic in our small coffee area and, yes, it's often loud, but it's an image of the Kingdom. After taking off my vestments the first things I see when I go into the coffee area are ten high chairs lined up with our little ones with bits and pieces of cake smeared on their faces, sippy cups filled with juice, and big bright smiles. If this isn't an image of the Kingdom I don't know what is.

By now I'm tired. The day started at six thirty and it's not over. I'm still on the clock. After taking off my vestments I have to *press the flesh*. Although I'd much rather take off my vestments and head straight for the door to my car and home. Being an introvert means that after a full Liturgy with a sermon and then the announcements I'm emotionally and psychologically depleted. I need time to regroup and rejuvenate, like a scuba diver surfacing after a deep dive, you have to resurface slowly otherwise you'll get a bad case of the bends. I can't resurface to normal yet, I still have to mix and mingle with the flock. I often pray that I get a second wind that lasts through coffee hour. I admire the more extroverted pastors who can go all day long on Sunday, something I cannot do.

I hear good news, teens finding their first job or being accepted into their college of choice, a couple who is getting engaged, or someone getting a promotion. I hear the good, the bad, and the ugly. I hug and shake hands, answer questions, make appointments for visits, and greet visitors. If someone walked off the street they'd think I was a politician with all the handshaking, backslapping, schmoozing, smiling, and kissing. Most people have three, maybe four conversations during coffee hour, I have about thirty.

On a good Sunday I can leave by twelve-thirty or one. There are weeks when I need to make a hospital visit. Sometimes I have to bless a house or meet someone for coffee. Some Sundays I get home around one thirty, but there are Sundays when I'm not home until four o'clock.

When I finally arrive home I change out of my clergy clothes into something more comfortable: blue jeans, a comfy shirt, and slippers. I walk downstairs, pour myself a cup of coffee, and sit in my comfy chair and read the paper. My throat's scratchy, my feet ache, and my mind spins: who was in Church and who wasn't, who wants me to call, and who wants me to visit? Sometimes I take a nap before making supper. By dinnertime I've already been up for twelve hours. I feel bad for my family who doesn't get a chance to talk with me until I get home, but when I arrive home I'm tired and often irritable. I want to give them my full attention but I can't. This is a constant battle, how to be present with my family yet also take care of myself, a challenge for all pastors.

At the end of the day I question why I'm still in ministry. I feel feeble and weak, I have no grand plans. I certainly don't feel successful. Compared with my friends in the business world I'm probably a big fat failure. Many pastors think that ministry is about butts, bucks, buildings, and budgets. The more butts in the pew the more money you'll have in the collection plate. The more money you have the bigger your budget. The bigger your budget the better and bigger building you can have. People look at the big steeple churches as the successful ones, the ones with the big building, large property, and huge parking lot. I have fallen into this trap before too.

Over the years I've heard the same rhetoric again and again. Yet no one talks about the role of vibrant worship, quality education programs, good fellowship, and warm and welcoming hospitality. I've visited numerous big steeple churches and they're certainly awesome and awe inspiring, but their communities can often be cold and unwelcoming. I wouldn't consider this a successful parish. Pastors need to be reminded that Jesus only had a three-year ministry, twelve disciples, one of whom betrayed him, and another who doubted him. doubted him. He didn't have a big budget or a building program and had few followers. He died on a Friday afternoon and to many was a big fat failure. Jesus certainly had a poor track record. But in the end, Jesus was faithful. I've learned over the years that we are called to be faithful, not successful, and I often feel like I'm failing that too.

CHAPTER 12

Saving Souls, Losing Mine

After getting my feet on the ground and after the initial excitement and thrill of parish life had worn off, I noticed Sunday attendance was sporadic. About half the congregation attended every week, about a quarter or so came twice per month, and the other quarter showed up once a month. A handful attended on Christmas and Easter. All of this disturbed me. If I was there every week they should be there too. I set out to change things. I planned to save souls for Jesus, never did I think that I'd almost lose mine in the process.

One of the less frequent parishioners was Luda. She was Russian, as were her mother, Anna, and her son, Dmitri. At one point I made a note to reach out to her. I wanted to convince her to be a more regular churchgoer. I would get her to devote her time and talents. I thought that if Luda became invested in our parish community, maybe other less frequent attendees would become more active. I made Luda my pet project.

Even though it wasn't January, I offered to bless her house, which is not that uncommon. Parishioners sometimes have their house blessed at other times of the year. Before calling Luda I thought that if I invited Dmitri to serve as an Altar server I could win over the entire family, catch one fish and more will come. One morning I called and arranged for a day and time to visit. She accepted.

It was a cool sunny Carolina morning. The long, hot, humid summer was well behind us and Halloween and Thanksgiving would be coming soon. I pulled up to her subdivision, one of the many with stately brick homes and street names like Lilac Lane, Forsythia Court, and Cherry Blossom Way. I found her home not too far from the entrance and parked my car in the driveway. I walked up the freshly groomed lawn and wall of wild roses, and rang the doorbell. Luda spoke broken English and her mother couldn't speak any English. We generally communicated with hand signals or facial expressions. A little patience went a long way. Luda answered the door.

Walking into the foyer I smelled onions, garlic, and sage, not smells you'd expect for nine o'clock in the morning. We walked a little farther into the main part of the house and on my right was the dining room with three places beautifully arranged: fine china dinner plates, glasses for water, and coffee cups resting on saucers. On the sideboard under a large rectangular mirror were two large pies and a bowl of fresh fruit. I assumed they were having lunch or dinner guests later that day. We went into the kitchen, Luda had arranged the table for the home blessing: a white lace tablecloth upon which she'd placed a yellow candle in a holder, a smallish icon of the Virgin Mary, and a cereal bowl full of holy water. Next to the icon she placed two pieces of paper, one with a list of living family members and the other with a list of departed members. Anna was standing at the stove with her apron, stirring a big stockpot full of something. "Good morning," I said. Anna waved to me with her free hand, saying something to Luda in Russian. "Mama says good morning," Luda said. I reached into my clergy bag and took out my stole and placed it over my head and started. The prayer service is short, most of it is taken up by the blessing itself. I walked around the house sprinkling holy water in each room while singing the main hymn for Epiphany:

> When thou O Lord wast baptized in the Jordan,
> The worship of the Trinity was made manifest.
> For the voice, of the Father bare witness to thee
> And called thee his beloved Son.
> And the Spirit in the form of a dove
> Confirmed the truthfulness of his word,
> O Christ our God who hast revealed thyself
> And hast enlightened the world glory to thee!

I removed my stole and placed it in my clergy bag when Luda said, "Father Bill. Please, please come. We eat in dining room, okay?" Dining room? I hadn't realized that we were having a meal, I assumed just some coffee and cookies.

"Oh, ok," I said, looking surprised. I followed her.

"You sit here." She motioned me to sit at the head of the table. Anna was still in the kitchen.

"All of this for us?"

"Yes," she said smiling, "Mama wanted to cook something special. In Russia, we treat priest like royalty."

I sat down at the head of the table. Luda had an eye for detail, she even put out linen napkins. After I sat down, Anna came out of the kitchen carrying a tray with Swiss cheese, Brie, and cheddar and placed it on the table. She immediately returned with a plate of smoked sausages, kielbasa, and salami.

"*Oh my*, does *that* look good," I said.

"*Spacebo* Father. Mama is a good cook. There's more coming too."

She was right. I did feel like royalty. The food kept coming. After the cheese and meat Anna brought out a basket of freshly baked dinner rolls, a small butter tray and a bowl of cherry jam, and a plate of freshly cut to-matoes and cucumbers. She also brought out a bowl of peeled hard-boiled eggs, some pickled beets and cucumbers, and a relish tray with black and green olives. Then, just when I thought she was done, Anna came out with the main dish, a large glass casserole dish filled with a baked quartered chicken swimming in butter and what was probably a white wine sauce with sage and thyme. Most breakfasts consisted of a fried egg and toast or a bowl of oatmeal and coffee. This was a feast of feasts; overwhelming for an early morning meal

During the meal I made small talk about the food and the weather, but then directed the conversation to Church matters, to see if she would take the bait.

"So I see that Dmitri is around eight or nine maybe, is that right?" I wanted to slowly reel her in. I took another bite of chicken.

"Actually, he's ten, although he looks younger."

"I noticed he is not enrolled in our Church school program. You inter-ested in signing him up?" I was going for the hard sell. This was do or die.

"We're quite busy. Schoolwork, soccer. Sometimes he swims at the Y."

I nodded. Next to basketball, soccer was like a religion down here. I had to be delicate. On the one hand I wanted to push her a bit but not turn her off, this was foreign territory I was venturing into. I was still rather new to ministry and wanted to shine. If I got this family to come then I could reel in others. The bishop would be proud of me and I would be the envy of other clergy. I could just see it now: Bill the Evangelist.

I continued,

"I'm not sure if you know, but Dmitri would be a great Altar boy. He seems well-behaved and we could always use another helper." I thought this would do the trick. If I could get Dmitri, I'd automatically have both Luda and Anna; three for the price of one.

Luda nodded showing me that she was thinking about it.

"We'll see. I'm not sure really," she said. "He's on the shy side."

"Sure, sure, I understand." I didn't want to push. "I was shy too you know. But you gotta start somewhere. Altar boy now, then choir maybe?" I wanted to show her the possibilities, like a realtor showing property. She didn't take the bait. I was determined to keep fishing. I just knew that at the end of this meal she'd agree to my proposition.

"You know, Luda, I was wondering if you ever met Nadia. She's from Bulgaria, I think."

"Oh," she said in a tone that said, "that's nice but I really don't care."

"Nadia is married and has two boys. They live over near the Church." I continued. I thought I'd push the Nadia connection to see what would happen.

"Huh," she said. She put a bite of food into her mouth.

I kept eating. The food was delicious. Anna saw me finishing my plate and returned from the kitchen with a carafe of coffee and poured me some. She also poured herself a cup. When she walked back she said something in Russian to her daughter and then took my plate. I was going to have to skip lunch.

As Anna cleared away the dishes I realized I had failed. Clearly Luda was not going to commit more time or energy to the parish. No matter how much I pushed, pulled, or prodded it wasn't happening. I thanked her and her mom gave me the wrapped cherry pie to take home. I hugged both of them and before leaving Luda gave me a smallish wrapped box. I got into the car and drove home, burping every so often from that garlic chicken. When I got home I opened the box and inside was a glass polar bear.

Most pastors are probably smarter than me and would have learned their lesson. They would have recognized Luda's verbal and non-verbal responses and moved on. I thought I could change people. I wanted to grow the parish, to show the parish council that they needed me. We could build a new building and a new hall. It would be a win-win loop. I pictured an overflowing parking lot and shoulder-to-shoulder sanctuary. Funny thing is none of this happened. There's a saying, if you want to make God laugh, make a plan. True. I had to learn the hard way.

I'm a slow learner. It took me a few years but I eventually gave up trying to convince people of anything. After much headache and heartache my eyes were opened. I had the wrong ideas about ministry and community life. I believed all of the slick Church growth programs that suggested that parishes pay for expensive billboards and create fancy websites and glossy brochures. I read about charismatic leadership and having a strong vision. I was trying to be like a cowboy, driving the cattle to greener pastures. I certainly wasn't acting as a gentle shepherd who walked ahead of the sheep seeking cool streams and peaceful pastures. I learned that no amount of cajoling or convincing changes anyone. At first people may respond and attend services a few times to make you happy, but they'll eventually stop. Their hearts have to change in order to have a deeper faith. Change, I finally learned, comes from within. It took a lot of failing and hitting the same wall again and again to realize that I couldn't make anyone change. It never worked. It never does. I no longer get angry or upset. Yet it took dozens of Ludas and Dmitris to teach me this lesson. The important thing is that I learned.

CHAPTER 13

When God Shows Up

I'm in my car heading south on I-85 towards Shelby. I'm listening to an NPR author interview, something about the Guantanamo Bay Prison. Civilization passes by as I drive past Mount Holly, Belmont, Dallas, Gastonia, and Kings Mountain. Here it's wide fields of green grass and spring wheat, an occasional warehouse or two, and antique and pottery shops. At Kings Mountain I turn off onto State Road 74 and head West. No more billboards for the Charlotte Panthers and Harris Teeter, here it's all Cracker Barrel, Biscuitville, Walmart, and signs saying that Jesus is coming again, as if we had to be reminded.

I don't want to be driving and I don't want to be headed to Shelby. Shelby is in the middle of nowhere. Well, it's somewhere, but nowhere most people would want to go. I'd rather be home reading a book or working in the garden or walking my dog. I know this sounds horrible, but it's true. I'm driving to Shelby to visit a dying woman named Mary whom I've never met. Her husband, Nick, called me a few days ago telling me that she had a procedure on her leg that led to an infection and the infection caused gangrene. After the gangrene set in, the surgeon began slicing off body parts, first her toes, then her foot, then her lower leg, then her whole leg. Now she's going to die from the infection. He and his wife don't attend my parish. In fact they don't attend any parish. They moved here from Pennsylvania, but neither of them drives so they are stuck in Shelby. They found me on-line. This happens throughout the year. Many of my pastoral visits aren't with my own parishioners, but with people like this who contact me in an emergency.

After about forty minutes I find myself at the intersection of South Lafayette and Main Street in downtown Shelby, which is reminiscent of many American Main Streets: vacant storefronts, for lease signs, an old five-and-dime, and a movie theater. Shelby is nowhere I'd like to visit and nowhere I'd like to live.

After a few blocks I spot the nursing home on my left, nestled in a grove of old oak trees. I drive into the parking lot and find a space near the front door. I open the glove compartment and take out a breath mint, fix my hair in the rearview mirror, slide a white collar in my shirt, and get out of the car. I've done this plenty of times already, but I still don't like it. It's very awkward because I never know what to expect. Visiting parishioners is easy. I know them and they know me. There is a common history and stories, we have an ongoing relationship, which strangers do not have. I never know if folks will be happy or hostile, emotional or calm. The front porch has an old-fashioned green wooden swing and three white rocking chairs. Below, in the planters, are purple pansies and pink impatiens. From the outside the place looks fresh and friendly.

Upon entering I notice the familiar nursing home smell: pine sol and bleach. Janitors use them to cover up the other smells, but the more pine sol they use the more off-putting it is. There are nursing homes that don't smell like this but they're the pricier ones. I visited a nursing home once and I couldn't tell if it was a nursing home or the Ritz. This nursing home is nice, but it's not the Ritz. After surveying my surroundings I walk over to the reception-desk on my right. She is somewhere in her mid-sixties with dark brown hair put up in a bouffant. She notices me and with her free hand shows me that she's on the phone. I read the certificates on the wall: local rotary club, Better Business Bureau, various food inspection certificates, and a framed newspaper article with the title, "Maple Manor: Voted Number 1 in County." *Yeah, yeah*, I think, they all say that. Number 1 in this or that. Let's be honest, healthcare isn't always about health, it's all about the money; the more patients, the more money, the more money, the bigger the salaries. It's one big money loop. Medicare, Medicaid, nurses, doctors, drug companies, hospice, hospitals, insurance companies, rehab centers, medical researchers, they all have their hand in the bag. And who winds up paying for all of this? We do. I've visited so many nursing homes, rehab centers, clinics, hospitals, and hospice facilities; they all look the same after a while. Some are nicer, maybe better-trained staff. Others have more activities and trips, but let's face it, people are waiting to die. You see it in their eyes, sitting in their wheelchairs lined up in the hall like airplanes waiting for takeoff. Some stare into space, some read, others watch television and some play cards. Once I saw someone sitting in her wheelchair parked halfway in the TV room and halfway in the hallway. Her head was bowed and I thought she was dead. After a second glance I saw that she was just sleeping. At her age you never know.

Thankfully the receptionist finally gets off the phone,

"Hi, welcome to Maple Manor," she says in her southern drawl. For a moment I thought I was talking with Scarlett O'Hara.

"I'm here to see Mary Hash," I say.

"Who?" She asks.

"Mary Hash. Well, I think it's Hash. Let me look." I look down at a tiny piece of paper where I scribbled her name. The receptionist probably thinks I'm crazy, what kind of minister doesn't know who they're visiting?

"Oh, sorry." Looking down, "it's Hotch, *Mary Hotch*," I repeat.

"Okay then. Hotch. Hotch." She says to herself as she picks up a clipboard and scans through a long list of names.

"Hotch. Room 61, bed A," she says confidently. "Make a right at the end of the hall, follow it all around. It's on the left. Good luck, honey."

Honey. I can't get used to honey, sweetheart, sugar, or sweetie. In Jersey, if I called someone honey they'd give me the *who in the hell do you think you are?* look.

I walk along the hallway and repeat under my breath, "61 A, 61 A." I pass by two more offices and then make a right. Now I'm in the heart of the nursing home. Walking down the long hallway is like navigating an obstacle course. A janitor on my left mops the floor. Ahead of me is a yellow caution cone in the middle of the hall, nurses pop in and out of rooms, one holding her stethoscope and the other pushing a medicine cart. Patients in wheelchairs and walkers slowly make their way to somewhere. The hall is like a four lane highway, each of us trying not to get in the way of the other.

Contrary to what people think nursing homes are not quiet places. Sounds, both soft and loud, emanate from the rooms—from low level moaning to laughing or farting, to the constant cling-clang of the phones at the nursing stations. The TV is always a few notches too loud or someone calls for a nurse. Odors are more profound too: not only pine sol and ammonia, but grilled cheese and tomato soup, or maybe it's lasagna? My stomach gurgles. Whatever it is it smells pretty good. It's lunchtime and I forgot to bring a granola bar for the return ride home. A nurse with gold-hooped earrings looks in my direction and smiles; another nurse to my left looks at me and quickly looks away. Perhaps my collar scared her? That happens a lot, people see the God-man coming and look away. I never got used to that either. People used to be happy to see the pastor, now they look away, not a great confidence builder.

I continue walking, I really don't want to be here. I don't want to be an hour from home. I don't want to make small talk with people I don't know. Even though I've been a pastor for a while now it's still awkward. I also don't know what to expect. Is the family angry? Will they be crying? Will they be in denial? Denial is the worst. It's hard ministering to someone who can't let go of Mama or Daddy. I always put on my pastor face, but, whatI want to say is, " Mom's eighty-five and has pneumonia, she's going to die one day, so what's wrong with today? Just be thankful she's not hanging around." Some people don't want to face the truth. They'd rather keep grandma plugged in so they can visit her in the rehab center and feed her applesauce and oatmeal. They want her to live forever, but grandma is ninety-two and won't live forever. Truth is it's about their emotional needs, not grandma. Our life is one big letting go. Pastors are in the truth telling business, but most folks don't want to hear the truth.

My hand tenses up on the handle of the clergy bag. I slow down when I see two men ahead of me, one older, the husband probably, and one younger, the son. Both have grey hair. I have arrived at room 61A,

I shake the older man's hand first, assuming that he's the husband.

"Hello, Mr. Hotch, I'm Father Bill, I'm so sorry about your wife," I say in a hushed voice not to draw attention to myself and not to make too much noise in the hallway. A nurse is walking in and out of rooms across the hall. I notice the door to 61A is open.

"Hello Father, so glad you could come,." He's dressed in baggy blue dress slacks and an old button-up shirt that is left untucked. He looks a little unkept but nothing out of the ordinary. He's slightly hunched over and looks like he's somewhere in his mid mid-eighties.

The younger man is probably in his late fifties or early sixties, tall with silver hair. He is standing near the door at a distance from the older man. Before I say anything the father speaks up, "Father, this is my son, Rick Jr."

"Hello Rick," I say reaching to shake his hand, "Sorry about your mother, must be very hard for the two of you."

He looks at me briefly, shakes my hand and then takes a long look down the hall. "Thanks Father, thanks for coming," he says in a soft voice. He looks tired. His father continues, "Well, Father, as I said to you on the phone, Mary's been here for three years now. They've taken good care of her, really good care. But from what the doctor says, this is the end. Gangrene finally got her. But I'm ready for the good Lord to take her, I really am."

I nod. From his calm demeanor and a slight smile, he doesn't seem like he's in denial. He acknowledges that his wife is dying so that's good. His son is also by his side, which is good. He speaks with sincerity and honesty. Judging from what little I know so far he's ready for her to pass. I'm relieved.

"Was the drive long?" he asks.

"Not too bad, although I wouldn't want to do it every day." Actually I never want to do it again.

"Do you live in Shelby?" I say looking toward Rick Jr.

"No, Chattanooga, Tennessee. Used to live in Atlanta, but moved to Chattanooga few years ago. Divorce. New job." There's no need asking further questions. One thing I learned in pastoral conversations is to keep the conversation simple and let people share information when they're ready. This isn't the time or place to have an extended conversation. In situations like these less is more. From what I gather he's suffered enough and now is having to watch his mom pass from this life to the world to come. His dad will follow her soon enough and I'm sure he's aware of that too.

His tired voice and the shadows under his eyes tell me this has been tough on him. "You staying with your father?" Although I'm not good at it I attempt to make some small talk.

"Yea, just for a few days then back home again."

His father interrupts, "Ricky is a salesman, his new boss told him, take as much time as you want off, isn't that nice Father?"

"Not many companies do that these days," I say.

There's a slight pause in the conversation. I don't know what else to say.

I look through the door and see two beds, one empty and one with an older looking woman with snow-white, shoulder-length hair

"Is that your wife?" I ask, pointing over to the door.

"Yes, Father, that's Mary. She's awake but can't talk, too many painkillers. Her roommate is down the hall getting her hair done."

I motion towards the door with my left hand and both the husband and son lead me into the room. I want to get this over with and get back home. The room is typical; two beds, crème-color painted cinderblock walls, two TVs, two dressers, two bedside tables, and two small cork bulletin boards. A pink curtain, pulled to one side separates the beds. The room reminds me of my college dorm room minus the pink curtain.

"Mary," Rick says. She turns her head slightly towards her husband.

"This is Father Bill. He's come to bring you communion. Okay?"

She looks in my direction. For a dying woman she's beautiful, with her white hair and light blue eyes. I stare at her face. Unlike most elderly whose faces reflect years of wear and tear; warts and wrinkles and flaps of skin and liver spots, her face is smooth and satiny. No wrinkles or liver spots. I hope I look good at that age. I quickly survey the bed, no IVs, no tubes, and no monitors. Her hands rest gently on her stomach. She's wearing a pink nightgown covered with a light green blanket. Her hands, like her face, are very smooth and satiny.

The son stands slightly behind me on my left and the husband is on my right. The husband walks over to the bed.

I look over at her bedside and see a tall hospital table on wheels that is used for food trays. I remove her breakfast tray and place it on her dresser. I wheel the table over to the bed, setting it between Mary and me. Reaching down I prop up my black bag on a padded chair and open it. I take out and unfold a dinner-sized red cloth napkin, which I place on top of the portable hospital table. Then I remove the gold-plated-chalice kit that contains the bread and wine for communion. After unlatching the lock I remove the doll-sized gold chalice and a spoon that is no bigger than my pinky finger. I remove the gold-plated cylinder containing a crouton-sized piece of bread and place it in the chalice. I pour a few drops of wine into the chalice so as to moisten the bread. Otherwise, she may choke to death. I can just imagine: *patient chokes on communion, priest arrested, news at 11.*

I place the spoon to the right of the chalice, then reach down into my black bag and place my gold-colored stole over my head. Before beginning I look down to make sure that I have everything. "Mary, we're going to pray first, okay?" She neither smiles nor frowns, just a blank look on her face. Does she know what's going on? Does she know who I am? Does she know she's dying? She doesn't seem agitated or angry. She's not moving her arms or moaning or shifting in bed. She just lies there still and calm. The more I look at her the more I can't believe how beautiful she is. In all my years of ministry I never saw anyone as peaceful-looking as Mary. Rick moves closer to the bed and takes her hand in his hand. This is a genuine act of love and devotion. I make the sign of the cross and begin saying, "In the name of the Father, and of the Son and of the Holy Spirit. Amen. Our Father who art in heaven. . ." Rick joins me but I notice that his son doesn't. Does he go to Church? Is he a believer? Not sure really. I just keep praying and try not to focus on the son too much, if I do I'll get distracted. The door is open and I hear an occasional moan from the hallway and the sound of nurses talking.

After we finish praying I take the chalice in my left hand and the spoon in my right and move closer to her face being careful not to spill anything. With my right hand I scoop out the tiny piece of bread and move it to her mouth feeding her like a mom would feed her baby. "The handmaiden of God Mary receives the most precious body and blood of our Lord and Savior Jesus Christ, for the healing of her soul and body," then both Nick and I say, "Amen." Mary takes the bread into her mouth and I notice that she has trouble chewing it. Now I am worried that she will choke to death. I quickly look over at Rick.

"It's okay to give her some water to wash it down if you want." I say. I'd rather have Rick do it than me, I don't want to spill any and it's more appropriate if he does it anyway.

The son moves behind me picking up the pink water container that's resting on her breakfast tray and passes it to his father. He holds the straw next to her mouth and she leans forward and manages to take a few sips. She struggles a little and then lies back down, closing her eyes. Rick wipes her mouth with a napkin. He then moves closer again and strokes her hair with his right hand, "It'll be okay, Mary, it'll be okay." I watch him look at her. I can't believe what he's been through; the questions, the procedures, the bills, and the phone calls. How many times has he left this room think-ing that it would be his last time seeing her? The love. The tenderness. The compassion.

A voice from behind startles me,

"Excuse me," I look around and then down and see an elderly woman with a jet black wig and silver eyebrows sitting in a wheelchair trying to maneuver between Mary's bed and the dresser.

"Oh, sorry," I say while shuffling to one side to give her room.

"I'm Margaret, Margaret Johnson," she says. As she slowly makes her way past me she stops. She looks at Rick then at me, and then at my black bag. "Are you her doctor?" she asks as she points over to Mary.

"No, I'm her priest."

"Oh," she says with a look of surprise, "I'm a Christian you know, found Jesus when I was a teenager." She takes hold of her cross on her neck and shows it to me.

"That's good," I'm not in a mood to have a deep theological conversation with Margaret or anyone else. The only thing on my mind is the long ride home and what I'll have for lunch. When people meet a pastor they either walk away, change the conversation fast, or want to talk about their faith journey. I admire their honesty and convictions but I'm not always in the mood to listen, although I try. Today I'm not in the mood.

"You see that man over there?" she points over to her bed and up the wall.

My eyes follow her finger pointing and notice a large photograph of a man and a woman standing together. I assume it's her husband.

"That's Howard. Howard, this is Pastor Bill. We were married sixty-one years," she says, "sixty one, before the Lord took him."

"Wow," I say, "that's a long time. A really long time. I'm only married fourteen, I gotta long way to go!"

"Yes it is," she says, "yes it is. We were so happy together all those years."

She then turns back to look at me, "Nice to meet you," she says as she continues moving over towards her bed. "Hope to see you again. I'm not afraid to die you know, I'm ready when the good Lord is ready for me. I want to see Howard again." She stops for a moment and fixes her wig with her right hand.

I wonder what life is like for these two ladies. One is leaving this world and the other is still very much in it. I look over to Margaret's side of the room and she has a pile of books by her bed and some photos on the wall. I envy her boldness and conviction. Her faith is much stronger than mine. There are days when I wonder if there is a God with all the wars, deaths, famine, and disasters in the world. I often wonder why some babies are born only to die a few hours later or why innocent people go to jail while the guilty go free. I hate the fact that we still have high rates of poverty and homelessness in our country yet the rich keep getting richer. Most of our tax dollars go for our military while our students suffer in low-performing schools with sub-par resources. There are days that I wonder why I'm doing what I'm doing. I feel like a fraud and a phony. Then there are days like this, visiting Rick and Mary, where my faith is strengthened again. They ministered to me more than I ministered to them.

Rick and I make small talk as I close up my bag. I reach into the front zipper and take out a small wooden icon of the Virgin Mary and hand it to Rick. "This is for your wife. I wasn't sure if she had any in her room. It's yours to keep."

He removes a small envelope from his breast pocket. I take it and put it in my pants pocket.

"I'm going to be away all of next week on vacation," I say. "We're going to Florida for Spring break, but I'll be home after that. Please call whenever." I reach over and gently touch his left upper arm.

"The doctors don't know when Mary will pass, but I have your number. You know, Father, it's hard, being with her for so long. But she has suffered, she suffered so much," he says, "three years, she's been here for three years. It's her time and I'm okay with it."

He has a genuine peace about him, something which you don't always experience with people in tragic situations.

"Ultimately it's all the Lord, Father, it's all the Lord," he says looking up. He walks me down the hall, my gait trying to match his. We reach the nursing station and I continue on. As I walk, I find myself thinking I hope I look that good at ninety-three.

I make my way back down the long hallway trying not to bump into the wheelchairs or the nurses who pass by. I stop to sign the guest book at the front near the receptionist's desk. She's back on the phone again. Rather than disturb her I look over in her direction and raise my hand in a goodbye salute. She does the same. I walk over to the car and after placing my bag in the trunk I turn on the AC. Before backing up I reach into my pocket and open the envelope. It's a check with a handwritten note, *Dear Father Bill, Thank you for coming and visiting with Mary. We appreciate it very much. Please use this money for your family. Love, Rick.*

God has a sense of humor. Even though I'm often agitated and edgy before making visits like this I always leave with a deep sense of peace and calm. I know that Rick and his son were grateful. I came at their darkest hour and this meeting, near the end of Mary's life, was important for them. God showed up today despite my selfishness. God showed up today for Mary, but he also showed up for me. Mary's quiet demeanor in her suffering, Rick's devotion and love, and Margaret's strong faith remind me, even briefly, that God still exists, even in an old, tired, smelly nursing home. Rick called me at his darkest hour and even though I really didn't want to go, I went. God still surprises me, even now. I guess I'm a slow learner.

Mary died two weeks later. I served the funeral. Rick was so upset at Mary's passing that he got sick and missed the funeral. The service was simple and Mary looked just as beautiful dead as she had alive. Her smooth face and hands looked just like they had looked when I'd seen her two weeks prior. The florist color coordinated the flowers with her dress: lavender, white, and pink roses. The interment was at a cemetery in Shelby only a few blocks from where Rick lives. He told me that he wanted her close to him so that he could visit her every day. Before I left the nursing home that day, Rick told me that he wants me to bury him too when he passes. He wants to be buried next to his wife so that they can be together forever. I told him that I'd perform his funeral too, even if it meant another trip to Shelby.

PART THREE

CHAPTER 14

Into the Depths

Tragedy struck on Sunday December 6, 2006, the date of our annual parish meeting. The meeting coincided with the feast of Saint Nicholas, the fourth-century bishop who cared for widows, orphans, and the poor. He would secretly visit his poor parishioners at night, leaving money, clothes, or food at their front door. Nicholas is commemorated in the Church as a generous gift giver which eventually morphed into the persona of Santa Claus. The feast of Saint Nicholas also meant that Christmas was quickly approaching and everyone was talking about shopping and traveling. Soon the Church would be decorated with red and white poinsettias and garlands. The sisterhood had planned their annual Christmas cookie exchange and the children were rehearsing for their annual Christmas pageant. Holiday spirit was in the air. So were the evil spirits.

Earlier that fall all rumors were floating around that Walter was not happy with the new budget, an item of particular interest this year, especially the clergy salary package. The tension was about more than just the clergy package. Over the previous few years I had numerous run-ins with Walter and Linda. While traveling to New Jersey to assist my should be mother's transition to a nursing home, word spread in the parish that I was derelict in my duties since I was away quite a bit over the course of the year, a situation which was unfortunate, but necessary. Linda would often call at the last minute before a service, telling me that she couldn't direct the choir, leaving me without help.

Walter and Linda were pillars of the community. Before my arrival at the parish Walter had established himself as a shadow pastor, something that often happens in parishes, but I never caught on. Father Hank wasn't around during the week so Walter had stepped in as a strong replacement. When I arrived I upset the balance of power. He and Linda were the welcoming committee, the hospitality committee, the service committee. They both sang in the choir; she was the sisterhood secretary and he was the head lector. If you wanted anything done you came to the priest for a blessing, but you came to Walter and Linda for permission. Over time I sensed the tension between me and Walter but was unsure what to do. Since he was my elder and had been here longer than I had, I kept deferring to him for advice and suggestions. After a while I felt like Walter was the *real* priest and I just wore the vestments. The salary package was the last straw. I never saw it coming.

When Walter found out I was going to receive a salary increase, he told some people that he would not support it. News travels fast in a congregation, especially a small one.

Our meeting took place immediately after the Sunday service. I asked a few people to arrange chairs in a large open circle so that everyone had a seat. Having circular seating meant that everyone could see each other and created an open atmosphere.

We began promptly at noon. After I made a few brief introductory remarks and general housekeeping announcements the annual meeting was officially opened. It was divided into two parts: part one, which was led by the parish council president, and part two, which I would lead. Sam was the parish council president that year. He started, "If you will please turn to page four, we will discuss the clergy salary package and the proposed budget." He paused a minute as people opened their packets and flipped pages.

He continued, "As most of you know, our deanery adopted new guidelines for clergy benefits and we received the guidelines back in the fall all. The parish council has agreed to accept the guidelines." Some people were looking at their packet, some looking up at Sam, others looking around.

I noticed that Walter was whispering something to Linda. She nodded and flipped the pages in her packet. What was he saying? What was she looking at? I was distracted and stopped listening to Sam. I found myself staring at Linda, and when she looked at me I looked away. I looked around at the other faces in the room to see what they were doing.

Sam finished his introduction and announced that the floor was now open for questions, "Please raise your hand if you have any questions or if you want to make a comment. We want to make this as streamlined as possible." I shifted in my seat hoping that the conversation would be brief. Walter looked around and immediately his hand went up.

"Yes, Walter, go ahead," Sam said.

"Actually I don't have a question. I have a few."

"Okay, go ahead and ask away."

"I don't see why Father Bill should·be getting a raise when I haven't had a raise in years. Why should he?"

Oh no, here it goes, I thought. Walter had a captive audience. We were captive too, no one was going to make an exit now that Walter was speaking. No one wants to draw attention to themselves in a large gathering.

Sam responded, "The council supports it, it is good for Father and good for the parish. . ."

Walter interrupted,

"I still don't think this is right. I don't think the parish could afford the raise, not now, and maybe, not ever. Father Hank was fine with what we gave him, so should Father Bill." He forgot to mention that the raise was over a three-year period and they were paying Father Hank a very part-time salary, but I was full-time.

Walter's face turned slightly pink and he waved his hands up and down as he spoke. clearly he was agitated. I sat and kept staring in his direction. In the past few months Walter had made it known that he didn't like the fact that I had just received my doctorate, "Now that Father got his Ph.D., he'll be leaving us soon, a larger parish probably." I had no interest in leaving Nativity. Taisia and I had set down roots for our growing family. We already had a three-year-old and had recently had another baby. We liked North Carolina and wanted to stay. I had noticed that during the previous few weeks he was avoiding me during coffee hour.

As Walter kept talking, I scanned the room and noticed people sitting, staring at him. Did they support Walter? It was hard to read their body language. Were they against the clergy salary package too? Walter pushed ahead full steam. No one stood up to stop him. They were expressionless, I couldn't read their faces. Why were they so quiet?

I felt compelled to stand up and interrupt Walter. I was the parish priest and had full authority to move the agenda ahead. But I didn't. The more Walter talked the more I became passive. It was as if Walter was a male version of my Mom. When she got angry I closed down. As Walter kept talking, I didn't know what to say. I again surveyed the room and fix ed my eyes on Linda. She caught my eye and after fumbling with her papers she got up and walked into the coffee room. Walter kept talking. For the second time Sam got up out of his seat, "You said enough, you can sit down now. . ."

Walter interrupted, "I'll sit down when I'm done! I'm a member of this parish and it's my right to talk, *isn't it*?" Walter said, drawing out the last few words as if taunting Sam.

What started out like a series of small waves turned into a tsunami.

"And one more thing," Walter continued, "I also think he should be teaching the Adult Class, not Peter. After all we pay Father Bill, not Peter."

Walter was only partially truthful. I asked Peter to teach Adult Class, but only because I was busy meeting parishioners and welcoming visitors. Peter wanted to teach and I supported him in this new ministry. I wanted to encourage more lay leadership in the congregation and this was one of the ways that I thought would be good for the parish. Apparently Walter didn't like it. It's easy to take a situation, turn it around and give it whatever meaning suits you.

Walter went on for what felt like an eternity. I kept looking around the room, still no reaction from the congregation. No smiles. No frowns. No one spoke up against him either. Did people support Walter but were too embarrassed to stand up? Did they support the parish council? This was my sixth year at the parish. Many ministers leave parish ministry after five. Was this a sign that I should leave? I know I'm pretty dumb sometimes. Was this God's way of telling me that it was my time to go? Should I cut my ties and move on? Would I still be here next year?

Parish life has a beautiful side to it, people gathering each week in community sharing in brotherly and sisterly love and affection, break-ing bread, helping the poor and homeless, learning about the Bible, and growing in Christian love. But parish life also has a dark side that many people don't see, or choose not to see, and our annual meeting was one very dark moment. The Church is a hospital, a place where people come seeking wholeness and healing, and a place to work out their salvation. However, hospitals are also where very sick people go, people who have ter-rible diseases that kill and mame, like cancer and strokes and sepsis. There are plenty of examples of angry parishioners going on full-fledged cam-paigns against pastors, others doing everything in their power to remove the pastor from their position. They spread rumors and gossip. The Church can be, and often is, a very dysfunctional and toxic environment.

As Walter continued his verbal assault I felt like crying. Not only was he yelling at me, but no one stood up to confront him. Maybe they were all plotting to get rid of me and Walter was their spokesperson? Maybe my assessment of the congregation was wrong, maybe they believed what Walter was saying? Congregation members can sometimes be nasty. I had heard plenty of stories about parishioners stalking pastors, following their wives to the grocery store or calling at all hours of the day and night just to make sure that the pastor was in his office doing *God's work*. One pastor confided in me that a parishioner got up during coffee hour after Sunday service and said, "Well Father, one of us is going to leave, it's either going to be me or you, and it's not going to be me!" Before the pastor responded, two men grabbed the gentlemen by the arms and escorted him outside to the parking and told him never to come back again. Yes, the Church is a beautiful place, a place where you can find comfort and solace, but it's also a violent place, a place where people can be your friend one moment, and your foe the next. This shouldn't be surprising either: Cain killed Abel, Judas betrayed Jesus, Paul stoned Stephen, Herod beheaded John the Baptist. Why should my parish be any different?

I was their priest, their pastor, and their shepherd. This was my parish, my flock. I heard their confessions, gave them communion, baptized their babies, buried their dead, blessed their homes, visited them in times of sickness, and consoled them during times of grief and tragedy. I cared for them from womb to tomb and after six years one of the sheep turned on me. I never experienced anger and animosity at Holy Resurrection. Maybe I was blind to it? Did I ignore it? All I saw were bright smiling faces on Sunday morning and laughter and sharing in coffee hour. My eyes were moist. I couldn't start crying now; if I did I wouldn't stop. I had to be strong, or at least act strong. I noticed that people were looking in my direction. I kept my feelings to myself.

Walter finally finished and sat down. I quietly stood up and walked over to Sam who was still standing at the podium and whispered in his ear that he had to chair the rest of the meeting. We ended with prayer and I immediately got out of my seat and headed for the Altar so I could take off my cassock and cross. I was exhausted and just wanted to go home. Before entering the Altar I felt a hand on my left shoulder and a male voice behind me saying, "Father, do you have a minute?" I turned around.

It was Walter. What did he want?

"Yes?" I said with a sigh. I hoped he wasn't getting ready for round two. I couldn't take any more.

He paused for a moment and took a deep breath, "I just wanted you to know, Father, that what I said in the meeting, well, you know, don't take it personally. No hard feelings, okay?" He slapped me on the back as if the two of us were old drinking buddies. He was Jekyll and Hyde, friend one day and foe the next. It didn't compute.

How did he want me to take it: Metaphorically? Spiritually? Let bygones be bygones and let's go out for a beer?

"You did what you had to do." With that I turned around, walked straight into the Altar and leaned one hand against the wall. My legs were wobbly. I didn't understand. I didn't think parishioners treated priests this way. When Walter spoke he spoke with passion and conviction. Since no one argued with him I just assumed most folks believed him. Trusted him. After all they had known him longer than they had known me. I didn't understand how Walter could rant and rave against me for thirty minutes and then act friendly towards me later. It was too confusing. I put on my sweater, got my keys from the side table and walked fast towards the front door. A few parishioners wanted to talk with me but I said that I had to go home.

That twenty-mile drive was the longest I could remember. Thoughts came and went: images of Walter and Linda laughing and mocking me; images of seminary professors and fellow clergy friends. How did these other priests do it? How did they survive this, year after year? Was this behavior common? Did Father Paul have to deal with this? We never discussed this in any of my classes. No one warned me about the Walters of the world. I trusted everyone and thought we were like the Musketeers, all for one and one for all. We were all on the same side, we were all working to build up this lovely thing that we called the parish. Was God testing me or was I just too dense and not seeing the warning signs? Mom always said that when a door closes a window opens. The door to my parish seemed to be shutting quickly, but I didn't see a window opening anytime soon. I didn't remember driving home but all of a sudden I was at my exit, so I took the off ramp and headed home.

I parked the car in the driveway. How was I going to tell Taisia? Should I just say nothing and keep all of this to myself? I thought that she'd find out and I'd rather have her hear it from me than from someone else. There was no way I could survive in the parish, not like this. Walter was like a piranha; he'd take one bite now and then another later and then another later. It would be one long agonizing exit. I'd rather cut my losses and leave sooner rather than later. He also had a lot of friends. He would canvas the congregation for support. I didn't have the emotional strength to stand up to him. I was conflict avoidant and would rather flee than fight.

I walked into the house and peered over the kitchen counter into the living room. Taisia was sitting on the sofa looking through the Sunday paper for coupons. She must have noticed my body language and asked, "What happened?" I told her the entire story from beginning to end, sparing no details. I'm usually quiet but when I get excited I talk fast. She sat there patiently and listened. I think she was just as surprised as I was. She needed time to take it all in. I finished. I told her that I needed a nap. I walked upstairs, changed out of my clergy clothes, and I lay down in bed grasping a pillow close to my chest.

I woke up around dinnertime. Only Sam called to check up on me. No one else from the parish called. No one sent me emails. Maybe I was right, maybe they all agreed with Walter but he was the only one with the guts to say it to my face. Maybe they were ready for a new pastor. I went through the parish directory in my head wondering who was for and against me: Did they want me around or not? The questions lingered. I didn't know it at the time but my life would change forever. I couldn't undo what had been done. I felt powerless. I felt scared.

CHAPTER 15

Forgiveness Sunday Showdown

The period between the annual meeting and the first few weeks of 2007 are a blur. I know my in-laws visited during Christmas and I remember celebrating Epiphany and blessing homes as usual. Other than that, the rest is a fog.

I do remember replaying Walter's tirade in my head again and again. It was like the Zapruder film of Kennedy's assassination. Why did I let Walter keep yelling at me? Why didn't anyone stand up for me? Why didn't I speak up? Why was I so emotionally handicapped? People didn't see the Walter that I eventually came to see. But when I did see it, it was too late. I was left picking up the pieces.

Having a passive personality meant that I balked when he barked; I avoided Walter and Linda. Scientists say that humans are a lot like animals: they either choose to fight or flee. I chose to flee. I hated Sundays. Sundays meant that I had to go to Church. Sundays meant that I had to look happy and healthy and say something about God. Sundays meant that I had to put on a good face and play my part as the good pastor. After services I took off my vestments, grabbed my coat, shook a few hands, and then left. I became a good actor and made excuses, "I have to visit someone at the hospital," or "I feel a bit under the weather today," and left it at that. I avoided eye contact and tried to steer conversations to benign topics like the weather, sports scores, and current events. I couldn't face Walter and I couldn't face them. I was trying to stay afloat, but I was sinking.

I didn't want to talk about what happened, not with Taisia and not with friends. I kept my feelings to myself. I didn't want to think about what happened because it hurt too much. I pushed my feelings down and made sure no one outside knew how I felt. The poison started destroying me from the inside out.

I blamed myself. I became withdrawn, avoiding friends and family. I didn't want to go outside. People wonder what depression feels like. It feels like you don't want to get out of bed in the morning. It feels like you don't want to eat. It feels like you don't want to talk. It feels like you have a really bad hangover and no matter how many Tylenol you take you feel terrible. There were some days I just wanted to stay in my pajamas, knowing that at some point I would have to get up and look alive. There were days that I'd go to bed around ten o'clock but then wake up at two in the morning. I'd go downstairs and read, clean up my office, or check email. Around four or five o'clock I'd go back upstairs and sleep util seven. This would happen two or three nights in a row. I constantly felt tired and groggy. It was one big toxic loop: anger, self-blame, sadness, shame, and exhaustion. Repeat. I lost weight because I wasn't eating properly. One Sunday morning a parishioner asked if I had cancer. I said thanks for asking and walked away. I couldn't tell him how I really felt, I couldn't tell anyone.

The parish council convinced me that we had to act, Walter had to be reeled in; otherwise, things would get worse. They suggested that we write a letter to our bishop asking for advice. The bishop's terse response was that Walter would abide by the parish council or find another place of worship. He suggested that we have a public meeting with me, a few council members, and Walter. Someone should take notes so that there were both witnesses and a record of events. Everything should be documented properly.

The meeting was scheduled for the following Sunday. The Gospel reading for that Sunday was about Jesus and Zacchaeus. Jesus was traveling to Jerusalem and on his way he decided to stop in Jericho, where he met Zacchaeus, a chief tax collector. Tax collectors worked for the Roman government and, in addition to collecting taxes, they skimmed a little extra off the top for themselves. For Jews of the time, Zachaeus would have been considered a collaborator with the Romans. This Sunday was also the first of the pre-Lenten Sundays, which marks a forty-day season for repentance, renewal, and change of heart. Would Walter's heart be changed? More importantly, would mine?

During the service I kept thinking about the meeting. I stumbled over prayers and lost my spot a few times. Various scenarios played in my head: would Walter ask for forgiveness? Would he be friendly or would he be defensive? I had no idea what to expect. I wanted the meeting to go smoothly but I also knew that there could be trouble. Walter was unstable and who knew what he would say or do.

I waited for the money counters to leave the office so we could use the space for our meeting. It was the only private area in the Church building. I invited the council members and Walter into the office. We went through the complaints point by point. With the bishop's plan in place we told Walter he could stay at Nativity under several conditions: that he would step down from all leadership roles and just attend Sunday worship as a regular parishioner. If he couldn't abide by those specific conditions, then he and Linda would find another parish. Walter looked surprised, but he agreed to the conditions. Deep down I was hopeful I thought this was the end of my trouble. I was wrong. My trouble was just beginning.

Monday morning came. I was driving home from running errands when Mary Ann called,

"It's Walter. We have trouble."

"I'm on the off ramp, let me pull over. I'll call you back."

From the tone of her voice I knew something bad was happening.

I pulled over into a parking lot near the off ramp and fidgeted with the phone. She immediately picked up,

"It's turning nasty. Last night Walter apparently told people that you kicked him out?

Walter was out for blood. I imagined he'd do this. He canvassed parishioners for support like a politician vying for votes. After our quick conversation I just sat there for a while not knowing what to do.

Walter and Linda didn't show up for the next few Sundays. Every Sunday I looked out across the congregation and couldn't distinguish between friend or foe. No one talked about what happened. We still had our usual programs. For all I knew Walter had the support of the whole parish. When I asked the bishop what I should do he told me to ignore it, it would blow over and things would be fine. I tried ignoring Walter but he never went away. I later learned that ignoring things never helps, the situation just gets worse. This was my Waterloo. We were at war.

Life went on like this for five weeks. Five weeks without Walter and Linda. Five weeks of sleepless nights. Five weeks of picking at my food. Five weeks of moping around the house. Five weeks of wondering. Five weeks later it was Forgiveness Sunday.

In the Western Church Lent begins with Ash Wednesday, a day of contrition when Christians are marked with ashes on the forehead in the sign of a cross, as a sign of repentance and a remembrance of death. However, in the Orthodox tradition, Lent begins on Forgiveness Sunday with the Vespers and Rite of Forgiveness. The prayers and hymns for this particular Sunday highlight the importance of forgiveness and love, central tenets of the Christian faith. At the conclusion of Sunday worship it's customary for parishioners to ask forgiveness of one another as we enter the Lenten fast together. We go from person to person, face to face, saying, "Please forgive me," and the other person responds, "God forgives." There's a lot of hugging and hand shaking, patting backs, and sometimes a tear or two. Even though there's a lot of movement going around it's somber and serious.

As I turned around and faced the congregation to give the opening blessing I noticed two people walk in through the back door. Walter and Linda dressed in their Sunday finest, he in a dark blue suit and her in a purple dress. You couldn't have planned their entrance better. For added drama one of Walter's stalwart supporters handed her newborn daughter to Walter to hold. So there was Walter looking innocent as this newborn baby. I don't know how I got through the service. All I thought about was Walter and Linda. What were they planning? Why were they here? Would there be another public outburst? Was he going to confront me with his friends? I had so much anger in my heart, how could I forgive him? Maybe later, but certainly not there and then.

Would I give them a hug and forget about everything that had happened? Forget about the lies? Forget about the rumors? Forget about the annual meeting? Would they ask for forgiveness? Would they say they were sorry? Yes, it was Forgiveness Sunday, and yes, the Gospel is about forgiveness and love. Forgiveness also requires repentance, which means a change of heart.

I felt like the biggest hypocrite in the room. Me, the pastor preaching a gospel of forgiveness, but my heart was cold. I wanted revenge. I wanted to tell everyone how nasty and spiteful they were. I wanted to tell everyone how I was betrayed. I wanted to tell them about the sleepless nights and the sadness. I wanted to tell them how angry I was at them for not standing up for me. But I did none of that. I kept it all to myself.

After services I walked over to where Walter and Linda were sitting and whispered into his ear that I wanted to talk to him privately. Walter got up out of his seat and followed me to an inconspicuous corner in the room. I stood close to him so that only he could hear what I had to say,

"You know you're not welcome here," I said.

"We just had to come back, we had to."

"Come back? You got the letter from the bishop. You never called. You just showed up."

"Linda can't bear being away from Nativity. This is her home. She misses the music, her friends." Our conversation was short. He never said that he was sorry, never acknowledged the damage that he had done to the community. Never asked me how I felt. Never apologized for how all of this hurt our family. It was all about Linda and her emotional needs.

I walked out of the Church and was standing on the front porch when Walter and Linda approached me. After our short conversation I was surprised he still wanted to talk. I'm not sure how it happened but a yelling match ensued. I had never yelled before, but that day I did.

"Walter, I have nothing more to say to you."

"Father, you are mean. Just plain mean. This is our home. Our family. Isn't that right Walter?" Linda said, nudging his arm.

"I don't care how long you've been here. It's over. Now leave." For the first time in my life I spoke up for myself and it felt good. But I wasn't just speaking up against Walter, I was speaking up against my Mom for always telling me what to do. I was speaking up against Troy and Alfredo and Ray who teased me on the school playground. I was speaking up for other pastors like me who were pushed around by the Walters of the world.

A few stragglers were walking towards their cars and looked over at us to see what all the commotion was about.

After a few minutes I realized that this back and forth was not going anywhere. I turned and walked across the parking lot towards my car. As I put my key into my car door Linda yelled, "Father, you are ruining this Church, you are dividing it." I turned around, pointed my finger in her direction, and yelled back, "No Linda, you are!" After slamming the door I turned on the engine and drove home. That was the last time I saw Walter and Linda.

After that Sunday, life got worse, much worse.

The exodus began the first week of Lent. The choir director said she was leaving, but would stay through Easter. Two Church schoolteachers notified me that they were leaving too. One by one they left. Between Forgiveness Sunday and Easter twenty-six people left our small parish: two choir directors, the parish janitor, two church school teachers, the coffee hour coordinator, three lectors, and three acolytes. After Easter I wanted to leave too.

CHAPTER 16

Running From God

For several weeks I had a recurring nightmare. I was running down a never-ending dirt road. I kept running and running; running past trees, running past shrubs and flowers, running past open fields. I didn't stop. I wanted to run from Walter and Linda. I wanted to run from the parish. I wanted to run away from the Church. I wanted to run away from God.

Some nights I'd wake up scared and just lay there looking at the digital clock slowly change minute by minute. If I was lucky I'd fall back asleep. Other times I'd go downstairs and read.

One night, in an act of desperation, I typed a resignation letter to the bishop:

> Your Eminence:
>
> Christ is in our midst! He is and ever shall be!
>
> As you are well aware Nativity is going through extremely difficult times. After prayerful reflection I am requesting a leave of absence from parish ministry. Please accept this letter as my official request to leave. Please feel free to call me if you have any further questions.
>
> In Christ Jesus,
>
> Father William C. Mills

I printed the letter, addressed the envelope and left it on my desk. I never sent it. I wanted to, I really did. Every few days I'd read the letter and put it back down. It felt good just reading it. I felt like the prophet Jonah. God sent Jonah to preach to the Ninevites, but instead of listening to God,

Jonah wanted to get as far from God as possible. I felt the same. Where would I go? What would I do? I didn't want to be a priest anymore. Realistically, the only thing I could do with my credentials was teach at a college or university.

Drug addicts say that all they think about is their next fix. I felt like a drug addict. I wanted to make the pain stop. I wanted to escape. If I couldn't fix the past maybe I could plan my future.

As soon as Taisia and the girls left for school I'd go into my office and sit down at my computer with a fresh cup of coffee and begin surfing the web. I felt a rush of adrenaline. I'd first go through my email and then through pages and pages of academic job postings. The websites were updated two or three days a week. I'd check two or three times a day.

I scrolled through hundreds of job openings. In the post 9/11 world schools were looking for scholars in Middle Eastern Studies. While I knew a little about Islam, I certainly wasn't an expert in Middle Eastern Studies. My academic background was in Scripture and Pastoral Theology. While I could teach an introductory course or two in Old or New Testament, I didn't have the required language skills for upper level electives. I searched anywhere and everywhere. I spent hours looking through their human resources pages. No luck.

One day there was a job posting for a teaching position at a small Catholic college in Florida. They needed an assistant professor to teach undergraduate introductory classes in Scripture and in Pastoral Ministry. They also wanted someone with parish experience. A prayer answered. I read the requirements several times, printed them out, and gathered the materials: an academic resume, three letters of recommendation, a writing sample and graduate transcripts.

Like many people I hate waiting. I don't like waiting for lab tests or in line at the grocery store. I don't like waiting in the doctor's office. Rather than wait for responses I decided I'd just barrage schools with applications. I didn't care. I'd be like an airforce pilot on a bombing mission hoping that one would hit the target. I knew some school would read my application letter and offer me a job. Every day I'd stuff three or four brown envelopes and mail them. I was educated. I had experience. I was qualified. I deserved a job.

The day finally arrived. After lunch I walked up to the mailbox and in it was a large white envelope with the school logo in the upper left corner. I opened the letter thinking it would be yet another rejection letter. I was wrong. They wanted to interview me at the upcoming American Academy of Religion meeting in Chicago. Every year the AAR hosts a wide range of seminars from the latest research in Catholic Studies to Queer Theory and the Bible or Wicca and Beyond. If the topic fell under the umbrella of religion, AAR had a seminar about it.

I was nervous. I had been to a few AAR meetings before. They were large, as in five and six thousand people large. I enjoyed attending because I met some interesting people. Where else can you go and meet a Rabbi, Islamic scholar, and Baha'i minister all under the same roof? The big question was what to wear? Should I wear a shirt, tie, and suit jacket or a clergy shirt, jacket, and collar? On the one hand I was applying for an academic job so a tie would be appropriate. But then again, it was also a job at a Catholic college, so perhaps I should wear a clergy shirt and collar instead? I spent days going back and forth; clergy shirt or shirt and tie is all I could think about. I wanted to make a good impression. I chose a white clergy shirt with collar, tan pants, and brown tweed jacket.

I sat in a waiting area the size of a small school gym with rows and rows of plastic padded chairs. I looked around the room. The applicants were flipping through their CVs and dossiers. Some were checking email, and others were reading. Some were pacing. I was surprised at the wide range of ages. Some looked like they had just graduated, others looked like they were closing in on retirement.

I was confidant in my teaching and pastoral skills. I also knew that this job would be my ticket out of the parish. I'd get the job, we'd move to Florida and be closer to my in-laws and live happily ever after. I sat there fantasizing about my new office. I imagined it would have a large floor-to-ceiling window overlooking the palm-tree-lined quad. I'd sip my morning coffee watching students walk to class. I'd have plenty of shelves for my growing book collection, a wooden desk, filing cabinet, and a small brown couch where students could visit during office hours. I'd have a brass sign on the office door: "Dr. Mills" in gold letters. I'd spend hours in the library conducting research for my three-volume work on the New Testament. I'd have a teaching assistant who would bring me coffee and make copies. I would have a real job and a real career. Most importantly I'd be far, very, very far from Walter and Linda.

I also fantasized about our new house. We would buy a stucco Florida ranch with a screened-in pool, maybe a few Sago palms in the front and white and red hibiscus bushes and lemon and orange trees in the backyard.

It was basically signed, sealed, and delivered. I just had to get through this interview and I'd have a new job and a new life.

After waiting patiently for about forty minutes a tallish grey-haired gentleman walked over to my seat. "Dr. Mills, I presume? Or shall I call you Father?" "Either one is fine," I said. He must have been somewhere in his late fifties or early sixties and his silver hair was combed in a pompadour, which looked like a helmet. *Was that a hairpiece?* I thought. I wanted to reach out and touch it. In my head I called him Dr. Skinny. I followed Dr. Skinny to a little cubicle where he introduced me to the other faculty member whom I thought of as Dr. Fat. Dr. Fat's belly overflowed over his belt buckle and he had a double chin. They both motioned me to sit down on the other side of the small, round, plastic table. After the usual niceties and inquiry about my travel and stay in Chicago, Dr. Fat started with the questions.

"I see from glancing through your resume that you have some teaching experience. Can you elaborate?"

Didn't he read it thoroughly? I looked over and noticed that Dr. Skinny was flipping through some pages. Was that my resume or the next guy's?

"Yes, not much, but I did teach two intro classes at a local college. I taught both introduction to the Bible and an elective on the Gospel of John and one on the Apostle Paul. *All of my classes,* as you can see, were well received by my students."

I emphasized *all of my classes* since I had received positive comments from former students. Dr. Fat better go easy on those famous Chicago brats and beer, he was cruising for a heart attack.

"Not at a Catholic school, I see?" Dr. Fat continued, flipping back and forth from page to page.

"No, you're right. It was at a secular college."

"Oh," he said, looking over at Dr. Fat.

"You're not Catholic either I presume?"

"No. However, I have *seven years* of parish experience." In the Bible seven was a symbolic number, I was wondering if they would notice the Biblical connotation. I wanted to spin this interview in a positive direction.

"Hmm," Dr. Skinny said popping his head above the papers and looking over at Dr. Fat. I fiddled with my jacket buttons. What was he thinking?

Dr. Skinny started, "Have you thought about how you would teach New Testament in a *Catholic school*?"

Before I could respond he continued, "You know, most of our students are *Catholic*. They come from *Catholic* families. We have *Catholic* Mass every day. Most of our faculty are *Catholic*, especially in the theology department." He looked at my wedding ring for a moment and then looked away. Clearly, they were looking for a Catholic professor, although that was not mentioned in the job description. On the one hand I wasn't Catholic. On the other hand I was open to all faith traditions and understanding of a wide range of teachings and beliefs.

"My students were Catholic, Methodist, Lutheran, and Baptist. I even had an agnostic student who was one of my best."

Dr. Fat jumped in, "I know this might sound odd, Dr. Mills, but how would you explain to students that you're married? Obviously all of the priests on campus are celibate."

I caught myself twisting my wedding ring. Strike two. Orthodox and married.

"Well, in the beginning of the term, maybe on the first day or so, I'd just tell them I'm an Orthodox priest. Surely they'd understand."

Dr. Skinny looked over at Dr. Fat. "Uh, huh." Clearly he wasn't impressed.

It was Dr. Fat's turn again. "How would you deal with *Dei Verbum* in the classroom?"

"*Dei* what?" I said raising my eyebrows.

"*Dei Verbum*, you know, the Dogmatic Constitution of Divine Revelation promulgated at Vatican II. It's one of the most important documents on the Sacred Scriptures. How would you explain that?"

I had never heard of *Dei Verbum*, nor did I know much about Vatican II. I was a Scripture guy not a theology guy. Strike three.

My mouth was dry. It was then that I realized I'd forgotten to bring some bottled water.

"I'm not familiar with that document or with Vatican II," I said.

Dr. Skinny started talking. I looked over at him, nodding, but my mind was elsewhere. My face felt flush. This was it. I had bombed my one and only job interview. Clearly I was not as prepared as I thought I was. There was no way they'd invite me for an on campus interview. I wouldn't be wined and dined. No campus tour. No meeting with the department chair. No office. No tweed jacket. No teaching assistant. No sign on my door. No house with palm trees and a pool. Only a miracle would save my sorry soul.

They both stood up out of their chairs, signaling that the interview was over. I fiddled with my briefcase trying to distract myself from self-disgust.

Dr. Skinny ended the interview, "Well, thank you so much for your time Dr. Mills, I hope you enjoy the rest of your stay in Chicago. Great food you know." Dr. Fat nodded in agreement. Another pizza at Gino's and he'd be in ICU.

"Thanks," I muttered and shook both their hands. "Any idea when you'll make a decision?" I said before leaving the desk.

"In a few weeks probably. You can send us an email if you like, but it's a busy time for us.

"Understood."

I turned around and walked out of the interview hall. I took off my clerical collar and put it in my shirt breast pocket and continued walking down the long hallway through the revolving doors that opened up onto Michigan Avenue. I stood for a moment taking a deep breath of fresh, crisp autumn air. Groups of people walked past. A couple of men dressed in shirts and ties and classily dressed women with Coach bags and wide-rimmed Gucci sunglasses. I turned right and walked past coffee shops and toy stores. I replayed the entire interview over and over again in my head. Dr. Fat with his beer belly and Dr. Skinny with his pompadour. I kept thinking of my answers. Maybe I should have made something up about *Dei Verbum*, just said something, anything, to show that I knew what I was talking about. No, they'd know I was unsure of myself. It wasn't my fault that I wasn't Catholic. Even though I was married, the students wouldn't necessarily know or care. I kept thinking that I'd just wasted a lot of money on a hotel and plane fare. For what? A fifteen-minute interview that bombed?

Three weeks later, I received a form letter:

Dear Dr. Mills:

While we had many talented and strong candidates, of which you were one, we regret to inform you that we already chose a candidate for the position. Thank you very much for applying. We wish you well in your job search.

Warm Regards,

Dr. Skinny and Dr. Fat

Case closed. I crumpled the letter and threw it in the garbage can. Most people would have gotten the message loud and clear and stopped looking. Not me.

With my one interview over, I kept looking for jobs. Rather than moving, I thought, since we already had our house and Taisia had a teaching job nearby, I could find a job at a college or university out of state and fly out on Monday morning, teach my two or three classes and then fly back again Wednesday or Thursday night. I began looking at several apartments in major cities. I could fly in, take a taxi or metro to campus, teach my classes, stay in my condo, and then fly out two or three days later. I could make more money in a major city and provide for my family. If I stayed at the school till my girls got to college age they might be able to attend for free. I'd have summers off. Now my job was to find a condo that I could afford. Thankfully the economy plummeted and prices were at an alltime low.

Looking for condos took my mind off parish problems. I loved reading the descriptions too, "One bedroom walk up, fully furnished, close to subway and shopping. Includes doorman and some utilities. Granite countertops and seasonal water views." Or "Five story walk up studio artist loft apartment, plenty of light." I spent hours searching, it took my mind off the pain.

I didn't realize that no matter how much I looked for a new job the pain was still there. The fix alleviated the pain for a little while. Then the reality set in. I wasn't going to get a teaching job. I wasn't going to get a new apartment. I wasn't going to commute back and forth to Chicago, New York, or Los Angeles. Yes, it's one thing for someone single to live this kind of life, but not someone married with two young children. If I commuted I would miss soccer games and piano lessons, I'd miss school trips and school plays. The girls would grow up not having any relationship with me. Clearly, this wouldn't work. At the end of the day I was still here in the same house, with my same family, with my same problems. Pain hurts. I wanted the pain to go away.

The definition of an idiot is someone who does the same thing again and again, expecting different results. I was an idiot of the first order. No job offers. After months of looking I finally gave up. I was tired. It hurts too much when you keep hearing *thanks but no thanks*. It hurts when you've studied and worked so hard and have all the experience required and no one wants to hire you. I didn't understand. I had a stellar resume. I had written and published academic articles and books. I had given talks at conferences. I deserved a job at a big university. I had my meal ticket punched and was waiting in line, but at the end of the day my tray was empty. I was running in place and after months of searching I was in the exact same place I had started.

After I stopped my job search I talked to some of my friends in academia. They had offices titles and travel money and an office lined with books. They had summers off. Yet many of them confessed to me that they weren't happy. Some were actually depressed. They were overworked and underpaid. They served on committees that wrote reports that no one read. They had piles of paperwork. They endured long meetings. The economic downturn caused colleges to cut back on travel and fringe benefits.

It was then, after talking with some of my teacher friends that I realized I had a wonderful life all along. I had no committee work or reports to write. I didn't have to grade hundreds of papers and exams. I didn't have to deal with department drama and insecure colleagues who constantly had to defend their turf from other faculty members. I didn't have to deal with immature, whining students who complained about their grades. I didn't have a department chairperson constantly judging my work. I had freedom. I could eat lunch at school with my daughters. I could write books and articles, not because I had to, but because I wanted to. Yes, there were downsides to being a pastor, the loneliness and lack of deep friendships.

People try to run away from problems but their problems follow them. They think that running away will bring them happiness. It never does. Running away is a temporary escape. I realized that I had everything I ever needed or wanted: job security, a supportive family, great neighbors, and most importantly a loving and supporting parish. Who would want to run away from all of that? But I didn't quite understand what had happened with Walter and Linda and the exodus. Rather than running away from life I tried to embrace it. But it would take time and I needed help. Thankfully help was closer than I thought.

CHAPTER 17

The End is the Beginning

It's ten o'clock Monday morning and my first day at the Davidson Clergy Center. I'm sitting in a small beige room, unadorned except for a single bookshelf, a floor lamp, and two club chairs. A digital clock sits on an end table along with some magazines. The room is comfortable and quiet. It's so cozy that I want to take a nap. The window blinds are slightly turned so I can see people walking along Main Street, but they cannot see me. I play with a few straggly strands of material from the upholstered chair as I glance around the room, taking everything in. There's no turning back. I've already paid for the week and they don't do refunds. I feel like a soldier home on a furlough, not wanting to return to the war zone.

Ann sits opposite me, a stand-in for Betty White or Barbara Bush, but a wee shorter than either of them. Somewhere in her late sixties or early seventies, with cotton-ball white hair, a simple blouse, khaki pants, and Birkenstock sandals, she looks like either an aging hippie or an artist. What I call granola. Ann is my spiritual director for the week. I don't know what a spiritual director is or does but for this week I have one. This will be the first of two meetings with her. She has read my application so I do not have to tell her why I'm here.

We just sit looking at each other in silence. It's not everyday that people sit silently together.

Ann begins talking in a gentle, soothing, grandma-like voice.

"Bill, let's take a few moments to clear our minds and adjust to the room. Okay? Then we'll begin." She quietly folds her hands on her lap, bows her head slightly and I close my eyes. I don't hear anything but my breathing.

Ann begins, "So, Bill, it seems that you've experienced trauma in the parish. You must feel hurt."

"Yeah, you can say that again." I let out a nervous laugh. "Actually Ann, it's been really bad. I never saw it coming. It was out of left field and all, no warnings or nothing."

"You mean Walter and Linda?"

"Not just them, but everyone else. I never ever thought they would leave. Just up and gone," I say with a sigh while looking down at the carpet. I've noticed that I have a hard time looking directly in people's eyes.

Ann nods her head. I glance out between the blinds and watch a woman walk by.

"You're brave, you know, for coming here. I mean, most pastors don't ask for help even though they need it."

"Brave? Actually I feel stupid."

"Why?"

"Because I failed."

"How did you fail, Bill? Did you cause Walter and Linda to do what they did? They chose the way of darkness, you chose light." Now she sounds like Yoda.

"Yeah, I guess you're right. But I feel like I didn't act quickly enough. I feel like I didn't do the right thing."

"Everything is clear in hindsight, but it doesn't seem like it when you're living through trauma." She continued, "Most leaders will tell you that during times of stress and conflict everything seems murky, but afterwards the water looks clear. That's just how life is."

I nod back at her and look back down at my lap. She seems so confident.

"You're hurting, Bill, aren't you? I can see it in your eyes. The eyes don't lie."

She must have noticed I was avoiding eye contact. I avoided eye contact with everyone. I thought I might start crying and no way was I going to let Betty White see me cry.

"I'm scared about what's next, Ann. I just found out there's a petition going around asking the bishop to remove me—just like that. They plan on sending it next week. We just moved into a new house five months ago. We have a mortgage, car payments. What am I supposed to do?"

"What do you feel right now? Not yesterday, but right now."

I paused for a moment, "Embarrassed. Scared. Angry. I wish I never was a priest."

"Do you really mean that?"

"Yes. I do. I'm tired of being the leader. I don't know what the heck I'm doing." The fact was that I felt like I wasn't equipped to continue. This was unchartered territory and I didn't have a map or a script to follow. I felt like I was making it up as I was going and I wasn't going too far.

For weeks I kept thinking about why I'd entered ministry in the first place. I went from High School to college to seminary. My life was on a ministry trajectory from the beginning, as if it were pre-planned, although I never recall planning it. I thought that if I wasn't a pastor Walter wouldn't have yelled at me and pushed me around. I wished them dead. If they were dead they couldn't hurt me. I wanted out.

Ann shifted in her chair and then continued.

"Bill, where do you find the numinous in your life?"

"The what?" I had no idea what the *numinous* meant, my expression must have given me away because she quickly followed up with, "The numinous, you know, the Holy Spirit. Where do you find the numinous right now in your life? Where do you find the Spirit leading you?"

"I guess it led me here." I paused then continued, "Ann, I don't know where it's leading me but I know I need help. That's why I'm here. I'm lost. Really lost."

Ann looks at me as if she understands. She's probably heard stories like mine before.

She responds, "What do you think God is calling you to do now?" It seems like you need to leave the parish. At least that's what I'm hearing from you."

"Leave? As in just pick and leave? Where? I told you we just bought a house. My family needs the income."

Ann continued, "Sometimes, Bill, you have to follow your heart. It seems like your heart isn't in ministry. It seems your life might be headed in a different direction. We have to be true to ourselves. We have to be true to our heart of hearts and follow the still small voice of God. You have lots of gifts Bill, you need to use them, all of them. Maybe your time in the parish is finished. Maybe you need a new path to take."

"You mean, just quit?"

"Maybe now or maybe later. No one can make that decision for you. Not me. Not your wife. Only you. You have the power to stay or leave." Sounds easy for Yoda to say.

Ann glanced down at her watch, "Well, Bill, I see it's almost eleven. Our time is up now. Can we sit in silence for a moment and I can say a prayer for you?"

"Sure."

"O God of mercies and strength, be with your servant Bill, watch over him, watch over his wife and children, send him the peace and direction that he seeks. We ask this in Jesus' name. Amen."

Ann reached into her pocketbook, sorted through some papers, and opened up a small white envelope, took out a three-by-five card and handed it to me. I read it quietly:

> My Lord and my God, I have no idea where I am going.
> I do not see the road ahead of me.
> I cannot know for certain where it will end.
> Nor do I really know myself, and the fact that I think that I am
>   following your will does not mean that I am actually doing so.
> But I believe that the desire to please you does in fact please you.
> And I hope I have that desire in all that I am doing.
> I hope that I will never do anything apart from that desire.
> And I know that if I do this you will lead me by the right road
>   though I may know nothing about it.
> Therefore will I trust you always though I may seem to be lost and
>   in the shadow of death.
> I will not fear, for you are ever with me, and you will never leave
>   me to face my perils alone. Amen.

The prayer is from Thomas Merton, a well-known Catholic monk and writer. That card was either an act of divine providence or some serious serendipity. Merton knew very well the trials and tribulations of community life, having lived in a cloistered monastery in Kentucky. He was censured by the Vatican for writing about the Vietnam War and the Nuclear Arms Race and he and his Abbot, Father James Fox, didn't get along very well. Merton was well aware of trials and tribulations. Rather than run away from his problems Merton dealt with them in silence and solitude.

I never say *be blessed* or *have a blessed day*. However, after meeting Ann I felt blessed. I felt blessed that I had found the Davidson Clergy Center. I felt blessed that my mother-in-law, came up from Florida to help with the girls while I was at the Center. I felt blessed that Taisia didn't leave me after the parish unraveled. I felt blessed that Ann had given me that prayer card which I still cherish. When Ann walked out of that room, I knew that I still had no idea where I was headed and that was scary. I just didn't know the how, what, when, or where, but I knew things would get better. They had to.

George Jacobs, the director of the Davidson Clergy Center describes the center as a MASH unit for clergy: a short-term out-patient center that focuses on clergy wellness: mind, body, and spirit. George established the Center as a place for pastors to find healing and wholeness and equip pastors to re-enter parish ministry or to find a new vocational direction. They helped clergy, like me, who were heading towards burnout, blackout, rust out, or just plain out. Ministry is overwhelming and research shows that thousands of ministers quit every year due to stress and strain.

Pastors are walking time bombs. Many suffer from obesity, alcoholism, mild to severe depression, and often have troubled marriages. The irregular work hours, combined with always being available, results in clergy who are overworked, underpaid, and overstressed. Here's an example, from Monday through Friday pastors have flexible schedules and can carve out much needed time for prayer, spiritual reading, and sermon preparation as well as making pastoral visits. However, parish meetings are usually held in the evening, which is when spouses and children are home from work and school. On the weekends, when spouses and children have off, pastors are finishing up last minute sermon preparations, or conducting christenings or weddings. Sundays are the big day to shine. Pastors with larger congregations often have more than one service which requires that they return home late in the afternoon or early evening. Clergy schedules are not conducive to a healthy family life. Holidays are no better. Most people have off on Christmas, Easter, and other holidays. However, pastors, like police, EMTs, and nurses, have to work. Travel becomes challenging especially during Thanksgiving and summer vacations. Over the years I had to turn down numerous invitations due to my work schedule. Resentment and anger builds up. It's hard to *serve the Lord with gladness* when everyone else is having fun in the sun and you're getting ready for yet another Sunday service. Research has shown that chemical addictions, divorce, and marital infidelity are high among clergy, which shouldn't be a surprise given the sheer stresses and strains of parish life.

Finding the Davidson Clergy Center was just short of a miracle. One cold day in early January I sat at my kitchen table looking out into the backyard, watching cardinals and bluebirds perched on our birdfeeder. While eating my sandwich, I sorted through the mail and didn't find anything interesting, just the regular bills and some junk mail. While flipping through *The Christian Century* magazine a small black and white advertisement caught my attention: *Davidson Clergy Center A Place for Renewal.* I looked down at the phone number and address. I looked away for a moment and then looked back down again. Davidson Clergy Center? Davidson? I thought I was seeing things. There it was *455 South Main Street* in Davidson. Davidson is only three miles away and I never noticed a Clergy Center before. I put my sandwich down and took the magazine into my office where I quickly found the website. Buzzwords popped out from the screen: burnout, renewal, therapy, pastoral counseling, equipping for ministry, vocational coaching, and stress reduction. I kept repeating the words in my head, Davidson Clergy Center; Clergy Center in Davidson, Davidson Center for Clergy. No way, I *must* be going crazy. I clicked on every page, read all the FAQs and bookmarked it for later. From what I could tell the place looked legitimate and the staff members were credentialed and had degrees in their fields.

It would be three hours before Taisia came home. I went outside for a walk. It was cold but I needed to get out of the house for a while. I put on my jacket and scarf and took a long walk. Images from the website whirled through my head like a kaleidoscope: A place for rest and renewal; a place to get help, counselors, therapists, long-term assistance. I knew that I needed help but didn't know where to go. I had thought about going to see a doctor but what kind? I loved my doctor but she wouldn't help me with the parish situation. I didn't know if I needed to see a psychiatrist since I was having trouble sleeping and eating. Did I need pills? It's frustrating knowing you're sick, but not knowing where to get help. Ironically the help I needed was three miles away.

As usual I didn't wait for Taisia to come into the kitchen. I opened the door and waited for her in the foyer. I was like a kid waiting to show mom my report card.

"You're not going to believe this!"

"Bill, I *just* walked in. Can you *please wait* till I put my stuff away." I had the terrible habit of barraging her with the day's news as soon as she came home.

"No, this can't wait. You're not going to believe it," I said.

"Believe what?" She grunted, trying to take off her coat and scarf.

I kept talking. She walked past me and put her bags on the center island and hung her keys and wallet on the wall.

"There's a Clergy Center in Davidson. Can you believe it? Right here in Davidson."

"Where?"

"Next to that neat art gallery that we like, in the brick building."

"Never heard of it."

"Yeah, me too. Anyway, they have a five-day in-house therapy for clergy wellness. I called and they have an opening for the second week of February."

"Then go," she said as she walked past me into the living room. I followed.

"What do you mean, *just go*? You didn't hear the rest." I said.

"I don't need to. You need help so just go. Get help."

That was the thing about Taisia. If something seems right to her she goes with it. No questions or quandaries. Unlike me she didn't have to ruminate on it forever; I live in my head, she lives in her heart.

"There's a problem. It's five days, nine to five and you have to attend all of the sessions. I asked about childcare and they don't have any. What about Emma?" Hannah was in pre-school, Emma was four months old and needed someone to watch her.

"We'll figure it out. We can always ask Mom, she's not doing anything."

After dinner Taisia called her mother and it was a done deal. Mom would come up and watch Emma while Hannah was in school and I could attend the entire five-day session.

I was worried. Money was an issue. We had just moved into our house and bought new furniture and had new landscaping installed. The Center charged two thousand for the week. George said that parishes often give scholarships or help clergy pay to attend the sessions. I wasn't going to ask the parish council for help. I was supposed to be strong. I was supposed to have it all together. What would they think of their pastor going to an intensive therapy program? Would they understand? Or would they ask me to leave and get someone else who wasn't messed up?

George told me to show up Monday morning at eight o'clock.

We gathered in the large meeting room. There were two large sofas big enough for four adults, and then two love seats in a U-formation. Bookshelves lined the walls and there were piles of magazines on the tables. A small bowl of mini Hershey chocolate candies sat in a red pottery bowl on the coffee table. Off in the corner, near the entrance was a coffee maker, small dorm-room-sized refrigerator with sodas and juice. The walls were beige. I felt like it was the first day of school, new classroom, new teacher, and butterflies in my stomach. I didn't know what to expect.

Four pastors had signed up for the week. Two of us were roughly the same age, two were older; three men and one woman.

Our day was strictly regimented. Each morning we had a one-on-one physical training session with a trainer at the local Y, then time to get washed up and changed, and then an hour with a spiritual director and personal counselor, lunch on our own, and then back to the Center for group sessions. Afternoons would be devoted to small group work. Each day one counselor would lead us in discussions regarding clergy self-care, personality and psychological development, and family systems theory.

Two of the pastors were navigating their retirement. They wanted to end well. I was envious. They were leaving and looking forward to visiting grandkids, playing golf and tennis, taking long afternoon naps, reading, and traveling.

Two of us were dealing with trauma. The other pastor could have been my twin. We were the same age and had been in ministry for the same amount of time. We both had young children. Before coming to the Center I thought I had it bad. Yet after hearing his story I realized that he'd had it worse than I had. The counselor invited each of us to tell our stories. In telling our stories we would gain insight and self-knowledge as well as some empathy and compassion. We would learn about the other pastors and they would learn about us. We had to own our story before we could find the healing that we needed.

Ann was right about the eyes. The eyes don't lie. My twin's eyes were empty, as if a part of him was missing. He told us that he was taking several medications and he was clearly overweight. He confessed that eating calmed him down, made him feel better. He started crying. It takes a lot for a man to cry, especially in a group of people. He suffered from bullies in the parish. People think that bullies exist only on the school playground. Wrong. Bullies can be found anywhere, at home, at work, or at Church. They're sometimes called clergy killers or alligators because they prey on pastors. Like alligators they spend most of their time under the radar and seem like most everyone else, until they start attacking the pastor. It's usually never one big bite but little bites at a time, a little here and a little there making little cuts until eventually they devour their prey. Research shows that clergy killers often have a combination of psychological and social behavioral issues and fixate on the pastor. Some project their anger or resentment towards their biological father onto the pastor, sometimes it's jealousy, or other power and authority issues. Some clergy killers suffer from narcissistic personality disorder and will do anything to garner public attention and admiration. After all, a congregation is the perfect setting for a narcissist, they have a built-in audience. They are jealous of the pastor and want to take the limelight all for themselves. They want to be the center of attention. Clergy killers and alligators cause irreparable harm to both pastors and parishes. Their behavior is like a cancer that destroys a community from the inside. Some are consciously aware of what they are doing, others act out of immature personality development and are not aware of their negative behaviors. But in the end it's all the same, one big toxic mess.

This is a real problem in the Church that no one wants to acknowledge. One colleague of mine had a meeting with a member of the parish council. The priest was doing a fine job but one council member thought otherwise. He came to the meeting with a single sheet with twenty items of things that the pastor was doing wrong: from spending too much time at the local college ministry center to preaching too long. The council member didn't like the way the pastor's children behaved during Church services or that his wife always came late. After about a month the council wanted to reduce his salary as a way to punish him. Another friend's wife was under scrutiny because the couple had purchased their own furniture and had the rectory furniture put into safe storage in the attic. This handful of people wanted to see their furniture when they visited the rectory.

Alligators lash out in micro-aggressions on a regular basis, or sometimes it turns into a full-fledged campaign against the pastor and his or her family. Some pastors have complained of parishioners calling all hours of the day and others are stalked on social media. Some leave parish ministry altogether. Many wind up with marital issues, some wind up eventually getting divorced.

Pastors are trained to be nice. We're taught to smile and shake hands and listen and be attentive. We're not trained to deal with alligators and bullies. We're not taught how to deal with community conflict. It's one thing to fix a leaky faucet and quite another to deal with a major campaign against you. Bishops and diocesan administrators often don't know what to do. They keep sending good pastors into the line of fire and then they question when things go haywire. It's all very sad. It winds up being a lose-lose situation.

My twin and I were dealing with alligators and by the looks of him he was done. He and his wife were ready to quit parish ministry. All we were trying to do was our job, be the best pastors we could be. You hear horror stories from colleagues, but it's always about the *other* pastor, *never* you. However, this time it's about you.

One afternoon we were sitting around waiting for the session to begin, when I looked down at the Blue Book sitting on my lap and opened to the first page. I started laughing and couldn't stop. It was the kind of laugh to make my eyes well up, and if I had kept laughing I would have started crying. The pastor sitting on the couch next to me looked at me and I pointed at the first sentence on the page. He started laughing too. John, our group counselor for the afternoon, walked in, grabbed a cup of coffee and noticed we were laughing,

"Okay, okay, what's so funny?"

John sat down, crossed his legs and began sipping his coffee. By now we were laughing uncontrollably.

I slowly read the first sentence out loud,

"Warning. Parish ministry can be toxic to one's health."

John started laughing. Comedy in tragedy.

Someone once told me that at the ordination service pastors don't need a stole and prayer book, they need a hard-hat and hazmat suit. I agree. Ministry is as toxic and destructive as nuclear waste. Parishioners have all kinds of personal and familial sicknesses that they bring to you: family problems, sexual abuse, alcoholism, gambling, infidelity, verbal and spiritual abuse, neglect, passive-aggressive personalities, power, divorce, the list goes on and on. They assume that because you wear a shirt and collar you're supposed to have all the answers, and if you don't something's wrong with you. You're supposed to be nice all the time and smile even if you're not feeling like being nice. They don't expect you to have a bad day or family issues of your own. Of course our calling is to be of service to our flock and to care for them, but pastors are people too and we need care as well. We need people to ask us how we are doing or what we are thinking or how they can better help us be better pastors. But this doesn't happen, at least it doesn't happen as often as we would like. Few people really take an interest in our lives and our families. They don't want to hear about our doubts and fears and questions. They want us to be superhuman. Pastors are human and aren't perfect. We are full of weakness, doubts, struggles, and fears, and want to have healing and wholeness as well.

When I signed up for that week at the Center I thought I would leave all fixed and ready to go. I was looking for a Band-Aid and some pills, thinking I'd be back on track. I didn't realize it was just the beginning. I didn't realize how much inner work I needed. The week at the Center skimmed the surface. I left with more questions than answers, more mystery than certainty. On Monday morning I had a glimmer of hope that Ann, John, and Tom were going to tell me that the best thing for me was to leave Nativity, to find a secular job and leave parish ministry altogether. I thought they were going to tell me what I wanted to hear. They didn't. I didn't realize it at the time, but I had much more work to do. And it was hard. . .really, really hard. Thankfully I had Tom to help me.

CHAPTER 18

Tuesdays With Tom

Towards the end of our week we started working on an exit plan, a strategy for the next chapter of our life. My twin was planning on doing standup at local comedy clubs. The best comedy is rooted in tragedy and he sure had a lot of tragedy. Me? I had no idea about the next chapter, but I did know that I needed help. A lot of help. I couldn't do this alone. At the end of our final meeting I cornered Tom and asked if I could continue seeing him. He agreed. The following Tuesday we started. I didn't know it then but Tom saved me.

Tom was in his early sixties and looked like a college English professor. Like most counselors he didn't talk much about himself. He had a peaceful presence, a calming voice, and was always fully present when we were together. I'm not sure what he was thinking, but it certainly felt like he cared. This was my first time in therapy, except one session in college.

It was November of my freshman year, a year of tragedies: Dad had died the previous March, I had graduated from High School in June leaving my newly widowed Mom by herself, one of my best friends died in a plane crash in July, and I moved into the dorm in August. I hated my roommate. I hated my professors. I hated school. I hated life. I felt guilty leaving my Mom behind. Most kids gain the freshman fifteen, I gained the freshmen thirty.

Our dorm was on the edge of campus, which stood adjacent to cornfields as far as the eye could see. At night all you could smell was the rancid odor of freshly spread cow manure. I lay in bed one night staring at the ceiling. My life was coming undone. I was unmoored. I had no direction. I lay there in bed and contemplated ending my life. Gun? Didn't have one, but the guy down the hall was a hunter and said he had one at home. I could borrow his. Slit my wrists? Yes, but all I had was a disposable razor. Messy. Pills? Only had Tylenol. Drowning? Perhaps, but too freaky. Asphyxiation? No car, but I could borrow a friend's. Hanging? I had a few ties in my closet but no rope. My options were limited as they whirled around in my head. Each time I felt worse than before. I had these thoughts regularly. I fantasized how easy it would be to escape life, just one shot to the head or one deep cut in the wrist and I'd be gone. No more pain. No more tears. No more tragedy. But in the end I couldn't do it. What a chicken shit. Couldn't even kill myself. I turned over and cried into the pillow. I had many suicidal thoughts that Fall. They came as soon as the sun went down. I wanted to melt into the floor and go away. I wanted something to stop the pain.

I walked over to the counseling center and asked to see a therapist. He kept looking at me and I at him. He didn't ask me any questions and I really didn't know what to say. There was no script to follow, no prodding, no way to know how much I should tell him. I mumbled a few things and after fifty minutes got up and left. I never went back.

Before meeting Tom my idea of a shrink was a short bearded old man wearing a tweed jacket with elbow pads, sitting in a club chair with hunting pictures on the walls. He'd be smoking a pipe and speak with a German accent and talk a lot about sex. Tom was none of these things, although he did have a few nature pictures on the wall and a lot of bookshelves. He also had five clocks, three analog and two digital.

One day in a low moment I asked,

"Tom, am I crazy?"

He looked up from his pad, took a sip of coffee and looked me straight in the eye,

"No, you're not crazy."

"How do you know? Maybe you're just telling me that to make me feel better? Don't shrinks do that, make people feel better?"

"Let me put it this way. Crazy people do crazy shit, blow up things and strangle people with piano wire. You just have a touch of anxiety."

He took another sip of coffee.

I loved Tom for his brutal honesty. He was so *matter of fact*. He reminded me of an old salty sergeant who had seen a lot of battles. If nothing else Tom would tell me the truth. Everyone needs a Tom in their corner, someone to walk the narrow path with.

"But I feel like my life's coming undone. I feel directionless, not going anywhere."

"That's normal. A lot of people feel this way. Hell man, you've been through a lot. You need time and space to work things out."

"Really?

"Trust me on this one."

Trust him. That's what he said. Trust him. I guess he was right. After all, he's been doing this nearly as long as I've been alive.

Therapy was exhausting. Our meetings expended a lot of emotional and psychic energy and I left tired and depleted. I scheduled sessions in the morning so that I could take a long walk just to process what we had talked about. I would review my notes, do some journaling at a café, and often take a nap.

Some time early during my time with Tom, I learned about a family secret. Every family has secrets. Maybe you have an aunt who has one too many cocktails at Christmas, but then you later learn she has one too many cocktails every day. Or maybe you have a cousin who always shows up at family gatherings with bruise marks on her arm, but then you find out its not about an accident, her husband hits her. We all have family secrets we just don't want to talk about them. The problem, I found out, was that my family secret didn't involve an uncle or an aunt, my secret involved my father.

One day I called Aunt Natalie. Her husband was my father's brother and I was very close to both of them. During our conversation we were talking about my father,

"It's too bad, Billy, about Donnie, he suffered a lot."

"Whaddya mean suffer Nat? Dad never said anything about suffering."

"Your Mom never told you about your dad's problem?"

"No," I said.

"Billy, Donnie was sick for a while, real sick. It was bad," She said in a serious tone.

"What kind of sick?"

"Like in-the-head sick."

Her tone of voice shifted and the subject matter piqued my interest. I could tell this was going to be a long conversation.

"Oh, I'm not sure you want to hear it all."

"Hear it? Of course I want to hear it. I have all day." Aunt Nat was in her mid-eighties and I had no idea how long she would be among the living. I walked over to the countertop, poured myself a cup of coffee and sat on the screened porch in the back of the house. It was late April and our honeysuckle bushes were blooming and birds were chirping. She continued, "After grandpa Mills died Nanna Mills had such a rough time. You know, Donnie was home and she had to take care of that big house and the grounds. Anyway, a few years after grandpa Mills died, Nanna was acting funny."

"Whaddya mean funny?"

"One day Donnie came home from football practice and Nanna had the dining room table set for twelve, can you imagine? Dishes, plates, silverware linen napkins, wine glasses, even flowers. She was such the entertainer, not sure your dad ever told you."

"No, never. "

"Oh yeah. She was Martha Stewart before there was a Martha Stewart." She laughed.

"Go on."

"Anyway, Donnie saw the table set and said, "Ma, who's coming to dinner tonight?" And she said, "Oh just a few friends.""

"No one was coming to dinner, Billy, it was just the two of them. Then other things happened. She forgot to put things away or forgot to put the lights out at night. Now they call it Alzheimer's, but back then we just called it dementia. Donnie of course couldn't take care of her, so Aunt Dorothy took her in. When Nanna left for California Donnie came and lived with us. Uncle Kenny fixed up the basement for him."

"So what happened?"

"Well, then your dad started acting funny."

A simple question was leading to a conversation that I was nervous about continuing. Part of me wanted to hang up the phone and part of me wanted to keep going.

"If Bonnie was telling a joke we'd all laugh, but Donnie just sat there with a blank look like he didn't get it or something. Or there were other times when Kenny went downstairs and found Donnie just sitting on his bed staring at the wall. Once Kenny found him in his room crying. We were all scared." She paused for a moment and said, "Billy, you still there?"

"Yeah, Nat. I was just thinking, that's all."

I couldn't believe what I was hearing. I was scared. It was as if I were in the doctor's office, "Sorry sir, there's nothing more we can do." You hear words but you don't understand. At least not fully. Your life has just changed. There's no going back. There's no reversal of a terminal diagnosis. You learn to *deal* with your life going forward. Now that Aunt Nat was talking she had to tell me the rest of the story.

"I know, it must be a shock, all this, all at once. I'm sorry."

I had a small spiral notebook next to my chair so I opened it and started jotting down notes.

"So what happened after you and Kenny noticed dad acting strange."

"Well, I was beside myself. We loved Donnie like one of our own, you know, he and Bonnie were almost the same age. We found a hospital in New York, right on the Hudson."

"You mean a mental hospital?"

"Yeah, but back then they called it a convalescent home."

"Do you remember the name?"

"Oh it was so long ago." There was a slight pause on her end and then she continued, "I don't, I'm so sorry, I wish I did though."

I looked down at the words I scribbled, Mental hospital. Dad. Illness. Breakdown. New York.

"Did you and Kenny visit?"

"No, we couldn't, no visitors were allowed."

I then wrote down ALONE in caps.

"Sorry Billy, I can't tell you more, wish I could." I wished she could have too. I wanted to hear more. I wanted to know how my dad felt. I wanted to know about his illness.

After hanging up I just sat there on the back porch looking out over the grass into the woods. Young tomato plants were starting to push out little yellow flower buds. A cardinal sat at one of the birdfeeders pecking away at sunflower seeds. A light breeze came through the porch. I stared down at my notebook and looked at my notes.

I walked into my office and after a few Google searches I found it: Stonewall Lodge Psychiatric Hospital. From the picture it looked like an old-fashioned Tudor-style English mansion with hand-hewn rocks and an expansive country lawn.

I called the hospital and told them the highlights of my story. They told me that all the records were destroyed, but they kept the patient intake cards. They could send me his card if they could still find it. About a week later an envelope arrived. Part of me wanted to open it, another part wanted to throw it away, and another part of me wanted to put it on my desk and stare at it. It was a strange feeling knowing that this envelope contained news about a very dark time in my dad's life.

I opened it up. On a 3x5 white index card was my dad's name typed in the center with his birthday, the doctor's name and the diagnosis in big bold letters: SCHIZOPHRENIA and ECT. I had never heard the words schizophrenia and dad together in the same sentence. This had to be wrong. I got up from my chair and walked into the kitchen. My father had schizophrenia and no one told me? Did mom know all along and was too embarrassed to tell me? I didn't know what ECT meant. I looked it up online: *electro convulsive therapy*, otherwise known as electro shock therapy. His brain was fried.

I had visions of Jack Nicolson in *One Flew Over the Cuckoos Nest* in a white straightjacket yelling at the top of his lungs. I envisioned my father being strapped into a chair every day with doctors applying electrodes to his forehead and sending high voltage electricity through his cranium. I saw him sitting in an Adirondack chair staring out over the Hudson River. I saw him wearing teal hospital pajamas walking down the hall in a fog not knowing where he was going. I saw him lying on his bed day after day with no one to visit him. Here I was a grown man, ashamed to talk with Tom once a week, and there dad was zapped three times a week for three months. Dad never talked about his pain or problems. I was humbled knowing what my dad had to endure. I felt so ungrateful realizing how troubled my father really was. I always thought that I was better than him. Unlike my father *I* was going to go to college, *I* was going to get an education, *I* was going to seminary, *I* was going to have degrees hanging on my wall and an office full of bookshelves, *I* was going to be someone important and special.

At one of my sessions I told Tom about my father and his time at Stonewall Lodge, the ECT, and the schizophrenia diagnosis. I was relieved when he told me that before the advent of talk therapy and pharmaceuticals it was not uncommon for people with severe depression to undergo ECT.

When I was younger I had thought people who went to therapy were weak; strong people kept things together. Seeking help was a sign of weakness, a sign of brokenness. In seminary the underlying message was never show weakness. We wore the cassock and the vestments. We wore a silver cross and had the bishop's hands on our head. We were educated and had it all together. We were supposed to be strong and have all the answers. Never, never, never should pastors admit weakness.

Yet after my time at the Clergy Center and meeting with Tom and learning the news about my father, everything changed. It's humbling knowing that you're no better than anyone else and that there are people in the world who suffer much more than you do. I learned that it's more than okay not to have all the answers and that there are more questions than answers anyway. I eventually came to understand that weakness isn't a bad thing and that being weak is our greatest strength. I learned that many people get up in the morning, go to work, shop for groceries, cook dinner and make lunches, yet carry with them so much suffering and anguish. On the outside they look fine, but on the inside they're a mess. If they're lucky they find help. Yet many do not.

My mother-in-law told me I was brave. Ann told me that I was brave. Taisia told me I was brave. Seeing Tom each week meant that I had to be vulnerable. It meant that I had to talk about a lot of uncomfortable things, about myself, about my family, about the parish, and about the Church and God. I had to come to terms with my faults and failures and those parts of me that I was ashamed about. Yet at the end of the day I learned to embrace weakness. I had to relearn a lot of things. Eventually I came to realize that in fact seeking help meant that I *was* brave. I was lucky. My dad was lucky. We found help.

One time I told Tom what Ann had told me:

"I can't take it anymore, I gotta get out of here."

"Outta where?"

"The parish. It's too much. I'm overwhelmed. Ann said I should just leave so I'm planning on leaving."

"Do you have a plan B?"

"No. But I'll think of something."

He flipped through the yellow legal pad resting on his lap.

"I think you said you have a mortgage, right?"

"Yeah."

"Car payments?"

"Yeah."

"Two young daughters?"

"Yeah."

I hated Tom. I knew where the conversation was headed.

He paused a moment and looked up at me. I stared back at him and then with a sigh said,

"Well, I guess it would be irresponsible to leave."

"You got that right. Running away won't help."

"I'm tired of thinking about Walter and Linda and the problems. Why can't I just be left alone?"

"Look. What you're dealing with is normal. It happens all the time. Not just in parishes, but in business. We all think running away is the answer but it's not. The problems remain. The question is how you deal with the pain. You can't escape it. It's going to happen sooner or later. If you live you have pain."

"So leaving isn't the answer?"

"Well, it could be if there was something better. From what you told me there's not much going on right now."

"You got that right."

"So for the time being Nativity is all you have."

"Yes."

"So, make the best of it."

"How?"

"Most people who see me have the same problem: stress and anxiety. Problems are problems. Job loss. Divorce. Moving. Change. They all cause stress, they all cause anxiety. The root problem is managing the anxiety so that they can live better. Some take pills, others do yoga, and others exercise. It's all about learning coping strategies."

"No pills. Too many side effects."

"Well, you don't have to take meds. There are other ways to lessen anxiety."

"Like what?"

"Do what makes you feel good. You told me that you like gardening and biking, right? So make sure you fit those things into your life. The one thing I noticed about all pastors is that they obsess about the parish. They worry about membership. They worry about income. They worry about the future. All of this creates anxiety and I'll tell you something, it's not good."

I felt like shouting: *amen, amen, and amen!*

Tom was right. I obsessed about Walter and Linda. My life was focused on the parish and its problems. My life revolved around the Church year and the services and sacraments. I worried about the loss of income. I worried about the low membership. I worried about what people thought about me. I worried whether I had a future as their pastor. I worried that they might ask me to leave. I was a big ball of worry. I needed to focus on living again.

There is a common saying in ministry: is the parish your world or is the world your parish? My parish was my world. I lacked balance. Somewhere between college and my ordination I lost track of who I was. Yes I was a pastor and rector of a parish, but I was also a husband, dad, gardener, cook, nature lover, bibliophile, writer, and friend. I was a movie lover and explorer. I put my life on hold because of ministry. I needed to embrace other areas of life that gave me joy, otherwise the parish would crush me.

Tom and I stayed together for seven years, longer than most marriages. Seven is a biblical number. God created the world in seven days. The rites of purification were for seven days. Passover is celebrated for seven days. Seven is a number of abundance, a number of blessings. Every seven years the Jews celebrated the Jubilee Year.

We read about the Jubilee Year in the Book of Leviticus. The Jubilee Year started with the blowing of a horn ushering in a time for celebration and renewal. The Bible says that in the Jubilee slave owners released their slaves, debts were forgiven, food and money were to be distributed to those in need, and God's love and mercy would be abundant. The Jubilee was a time for extravagant love and grace. The Jubilee year was a year of freedom.

My time with Tom was my personal Jubilee. I was free from Walter and Linda. I was free from the problems in the parish. I was free from my pain and anxiety. I was free from my inner demons and darkness.

I was free.

I was free.

I was free.

I finally found my voice and it felt good. I began to live again.

CHAPTER 19

Facing Fears

I sat on the concrete pool deck. My forty plus years meant a few extra rolls here and there. It's hard to hide them when you're half naked. I scanned the pool left to right: an older gentlemen was swimming laps in the roped off lap lane. All the camp kids had just left, the water was calm and the sun was slowly sinking down along the horizon. Thankfully no one was looking in my direction. Hannah and Emma sat behind me relaxing in the white plastic lounge chairs, eating goldfish, taking a break from a long lazy afternoon at the Y. And there I sat, forty years old, waiting for my first swimming lesson.

For years I sat on a wooden bench at the Y watching my girls take swimming lessons with Ms. Margaret. Later when they became good swimmers they always invited me to join them, but I always had an excuse, "Not now honey, daddy's tired," or "Maybe later, I want to rest for a while." I got good at making excuses. During the summer I'd recline on a lounge chair soaking up the summer sun and catch up on some reading. If I went in I'd stay in the shallow end. My mantra was *two feet on the floor at all times.*

Something changed during therapy. Some of my fear was diminished. Before, I was afraid of Walter and Linda pushing me around. I was afraid of what my parishioners might be saying about me behind my back. I was afraid for my future with the parish. During my time with Tom I gained some self-confidence. I started to believe in myself again. I wasn't going to define myself by my pains and problems.

Ms. Margaret had been teaching at the Y for a long time and some of our parent friends highly recommended her as a swimming teacher. She had taught both Hannah and Emma how to swim, maybe she could teach me?

I walked up to Ms. Margaret, who was on the other side of the pool deck headed for the side door of the Y. I followed her and called out,

"Margaret?"

She spun around,

"Hey, Bill."

"Listen there's something I want to ask but I'm not sure how to say it."

"Ask away."

"I know this sounds crazy, but I never learned how to swim," I paused for a moment, "Anyway, I was thinking, do you teach adults? I only see you with kids."

"I teach all kinds of people. A few years ago I had an eighty-five-year-old lady who wanted to learn how to swim. It was on her bucket list. I have taught five-year-olds and fifty-year-olds. We can set you up whenever you like, we can start tomorrow if you like."

"Tomorrow?" I wanted to learn how to swim but I wanted to take baby steps.

"Don't you have to schedule me in or something?"

Mr. Self-Doubt was ramping up.

"Nope, I am wide open the next few weeks, kiddies have summer vacation.

She turned back around and walked towards the side door. I walked back over to the lounge chairs were Hannah and Emma were sitting. I told them about my conversation with Margaret. They both gave me a huge bear hug and jumped up and down shouting, "Daddy, daddy, daddy." I wasn't sure what I was getting myself into, but I knew I had to face my fears.

The next day I arrived at the pool. The girls played in the water, I sprayed sunscreen on my chest and dabbed some lip-gloss on my lips and followed Margaret into the pool. She had me blow bubbles under water and float on my back. She also had me use the kick board and told me to kick back and forth across the shallow end. I was a quick learner. It felt great being surrounded by water. I felt light. Margaret was encouraging,

"Come on Bill, you can do it, you can do it, just a few more kicks. You're doing great."

Then about two weeks later it happened. Margaret said those terrifying words,

"Today's the deep end, you ready?"

This was it. I couldn't back down now.

"Margaret, I'm not sure. . ."

Mr. Self-Doubt was working overtime.

"You'll be fine. We're going just over the roped off area, baby steps, remember, baby steps."

"But. . ."

Mr. Self-Doubt dug in his heals.

"Bill, we gotta do this, if you don't you'll never learn how to swim properly."

"Okay, okay. I just wanted you to know that I hate you."

"Don't you think I know that?" We both laughed.

She turned around, swam underneath the rope and came up on the other end.

"Come on Bill, your turn," she gave me a fake stern look.

"Now?"

"Yes."

"You mean, like right now?"

"No, tomorrow! Of course, now. It's not that deep here, you can still touch. You'll be fine, trust me."

"Trust me," she said. Now she sounded like Tom.

"Okay, okay."

I dipped my head under the rope and came up on the other side.

She was right. It was the deep end but it was still shallow. I could touch the bottom. She moved into the middle of the pool but close to the rope.

"Okay, you're going to swim over to me, stop, and swim back, got it."

"You mean you want me to swim to you and then swim back?"

I thought that if I played dumb she'd let me off the hook. Margaret wasn't budging.

"Yes, Bill, now."

"Okay."

I adjusted my swim goggles, took in a deep breath, and off I went. She was only about four or five strokes away from the edge of the pool. I turned around and swam back to the side of the pool.

"Wow, that wasn't too hard."

"I told you."

"Can I do it again?" I said like a little kid wanting to impress mommy or daddy.

"Sure."

I pressed on my goggles, took a deep breath and did it again. I could still touch the bottom but the water was deeper.

"Alright, let's move down a bit."

She moved to the center of the deep end. I moved along the poolside by holding onto the edge, the black numbers painted on the edge said ten feet.

"Okay, same thing, I'm going to stay here in the middle, you swim over to me, turn around and swim back, got it."

"But Margaret. . .."

Mr. Self-Doubt wasn't giving up.

She interrupted,

"You can do it, trust me. If you get scared you can always turn and float on your back. Remember, whenever you get scared, don't panic, just go on your back, it's the default position."

"Yeah, yeah." I hated her. She was good, but I hated her.

Right arm, left arm, right arm, left arm, breath. Right arm, left arm, right arm, left arm, breath. I was swimming. I was gliding on top of ten feet of water. Below me I could see the pool floor and the black lane lines. I concentrated on my breaths and strokes. When I got to Margaret I turned around and swam back. Right arm, left arm, right arm, left arm, breath.

When I got to the edge I grabbed onto the pool deck, took off my goggles and looked over at Margaret still in the middle of the pool.

"You did it Bill, you did it," she said, still treading water.

"I know, I know, I can't believe it."

"You did great. Make sure to keep your head down. Now I want you to swim to me. Stop. Then tread water for a bit and then swim back, okay."

"Okay, boss."

I swam over to her and then got myself upright and started to tread water.

"Margaret, I'm doing it, I'm not sinking," I said.

"I know. Can you believe it?" Just a few weeks ago you wouldn't even leave the shallow end, now look at you."

One of the most powerful stories in the New Testament is found in the gospel of Matthew. It was night and the disciples were fishing. Jesus was not with them. All of a sudden Jesus appeared walking on the water. Peter

saw Jesus and Jesus invited Peter to join him on the water saying, "Come."
So Peter started walking on the water, but the wind and waves beat upon
the boat and Peter noticed the wind and the waves and took his eyes off
of Jesus. Peter began sinking and yelled out, "Save me!" Jesus reached out
his hand and Peter took it. I was nothing like Peter. If I were one of those
disciples I would have taken cover under boxes and burlap, hiding from the
wind and waves. Thankfully people come to Church because of their faith
in *Jesus*, not in me; otherwise we'd all be in a lot of trouble.

Margaret was like Jesus. She called me out from the shallow end where
I was safe and secure, to the deepest part of the pool. She beckoned me to
come and I came. She encouraged and inspired me to go out to where I had
never been before. I was terrified but I still came.

One early August afternoon I returned home from the pool, showered
and gassed up the grill for some hotdogs and hamburgers for supper. After
a delicious dinner we sat around the kitchen talking about our day. Hannah
said to me, "Daddy, close your eyes, we have something special for you."

"For me?"

"Yes."

"What is it?"

"It's a surprise. Close your eyes."

"Okay, okay." My birthday was in January. *What could this possibly be?*
I thought.

I put both hands over my eyes.

"Okay, open them," Emma said.

In front of my place setting was a medium-size sheet cake with blue
and white frosting and red lines going the length of the cake. In the middle
was a little stick figure,

"That's you Daddy," she said as she pointed at the stick figure, "and
that's the Y pool. You like it?"

"Like it? I love it. But what's the cake for?"

"We're proud of you daddy, we're happy that you're swimming. Now
we can all swim as a big family, you, me, Hannah, and Mommy."

I couldn't believe they wanted to celebrate my swimming. I was
touched. I felt like a fool taking swimming lessons at forty, but I guess for
my girls it was a big achievement. It's not every day that children get to
watch their parents overcome fears.

Taisia took the cake into the kitchen, poured herself a cup of tea and a
mug of coffee for me, and we had that delicious chocolate cake for dessert.

No longer would I be afraid of the unknown, I was determined to join my girls for a long summer of fun. I was determined to live again. I was determined to enjoy the rest of my life.

Epilogue

Resurrection

One of my favorite scripture passages is Jesus raising Lazarus from the dead. Jesus' friend Lazarus was dead for four days. In the ancient world being dead for four days meant that they were really dead. There was no chance for the person to return to life again. After a few days the body starts to decompose, muscles, organs, and skin tissue break down. The body stinks. I've seen corpses that haven't been embalmed, not a pretty sight. After the events with Walter and Linda, I felt like Lazarus; dead, buried, and decomposing. I, like Lazarus, was ready for the grave.

I was worried that the parish would fold. After all, when a large portion of your congregation leaves, including lost income, you think of the worst. How would we survive? How would we pay the bills? How would we continue with our life as we knew it?

People are more resilient than I thought. Immediately following the mass exodus a parishioner came up to me quietly during coffee hour;

"Can I speak with you for a minute," she said.

"Sure," I said.

"Father, I am so sorry about what happened and a few of us were talking the other Sunday." *Here it comes,* I thought, *more people leaving.*

She continued, "I just don't want you to worry, we won't let them win. A few of us promised to keep coffee hour going, we're not sure how it'll work but we'll get it done. One of us promised to clean the Church until we find an alternative." She put her hand on my shoulder reassuring me. I couldn't believe what I was hearing. Maybe I was wrong. Maybe the parish was not ready to close yet. Maybe there was hope?

When Jesus came to Bethany to visit Mary and Martha, Lazarus' surviving sisters, they begged him to visit the tomb. When Jesus got there he called out, "Lazarus, come out." All of a sudden Lazarus walked out of the tomb with his grave clothes on. This is high drama, a person once dead for four long days was now alive. A miracle of miracles; Lazarus lived again.

The parishioner was right. People rose to the occasion. Someone volunteered to lead the coffee hour, another volunteer cleaned the Church, another volunteered to lead the choir. One by one people offered to help. Just when I thought Nativity was going to die I was proven wrong. Maybe it wasn't dying, but just on temporary life support?

As people stepped up to help there was a resurgence of energy and fellowship. We were in crisis mode and the parish wasn't just surviving, we were thriving. As people got involved there was more ownership and love shared among the remaining parishioners. Our ministries multiplied. Nativity was being born again. The parish, like Lazarus, was raised from the dead; we had new life. As people joined the parish they too experienced the joy and the love among the congregation. They didn't experience the trauma and the exodus like we did, they came in full force ready to serve and to re-build the parish: a phoenix rising from the ashes.

The events with Walter and Linda are long gone. Yes, there are the wounds, they will never go away. It's like the risen Jesus, even though he was raised from the dead, the marks of the crucifixion weren't washed away. But in the resurrection narrative the wounds no longer bear the same pain that they once did. They are faint reminders of one's life, of one's living in a world of pain and problems, of evil and darkness. My wounds no longer hurt as they once did. My time at the Clergy Center and with Tom helped transform those wounds, they no longer sting like they used to, but are reminders of what people can do to one another, even in the Church. They are reminders of brokenness, but also reminders of resilience and grace. In spite of it all, I find myself still among the living. I know many pastors don't make it. I'm a survivor, and for that I am grateful.

Bibliography

Braestrup, Kate. *Here if You Need Me*. Boston: Back Bay, 2008.

Brown Taylor, Barbara. *Leaving Church: A Memoir of Faith*. NY: Harper One, 2007.

———. *An Altar in the World*. NY: Harper One, 2010.

Cartledgehayes, Mary Jo. *Grace: A Memoir*. NY: Crown, 2003.

Holloway, Richard. *Leaving Alexandria: A Memoir of Faith and Doubt*. London: Cannongate, 2013.

Krivak, Andrew. *A Long Retreat: In Search of a Religious Life*. NY: Farrar, Straus, and Giroux, 2008.

Lischer, Richard. *Open Secrets: A Memoir of Faith*. NY: Doubleday, 2002.

Miles, Sara. *Jesus Freaks: Feeding, Healing, and Raising the Dead*. NY: Jossey-Bass, 2010.

———. *Take This Bread: A Radical Conversion*. NY: Ballantine, 2008.

Neumark, Heidi. *Breathing Space: A Spiritual Journey in the South Bronx*. Boston: Beacon, 2004.

Nouwen, Henri. *Wounded Healer*. NY: Image, 1979.

Pridmore, John. *The Inner City of God: The Diary of an East End Parson*. London: Canterbury, 2002.

Raynor, Andrea. *Incognito: Losing and Finding Faith at Harvard Divinity School*. NY: Howard Books, 2014.

Reidiger, G. Lloyd. *Clergy Killers: Guidance For Pastors and Congregations Under Attack*. Louisville: Westminister John Knox, 1997.

Richardson, Ronald. *Becoming a Healthier Pastor: Family Systems Theory and the Pastor's Own Family*. Minneapolis: Augsburg, 2005.

Steinke, Darcy. *Easter Everywhere*. NY: Bloomsbury, 2008.

Steinke, Peter. *How Your Church Family Works: Understanding Congregations as Emotional Systems*. Lanham: Rowan and Littlefield, 2006.

———. *Congregational Leadership in Anxious Times: Being Called and Courageous No Matter What*. Lanham: Rowan and Littlefield, 2002.